THE MALE SEXUAL MACHINE

THE MALE SEXUAL

KENNETH PURVIS, M.D., Ph.D.

MACHINE

AN
OWNER'S
MANUAL

ST. MARTIN'S PRESS   NEW YORK

THE MALE SEXUAL MACHINE: AN OWNER'S MANUAL. Copyright © 1992 by Kenneth Purvis, M.D., Ph.D. All rights reserved. Printed in the United States of America. No part of this book may be used or reproduced in any manner whatsoever without written permission except in the case of brief quotations embodied in critical articles or reviews. For information, address St. Martin's Press, 175 Fifth Avenue, New York, N.Y. 10010.

Design by Judith A. Stagnitto

Library of Congress Cataloging-in-Publication Data

Purvis, Kenneth.
    The male sexual machine: an owner's manual / Kenneth Purvis.
        p. cm.
    ISBN 0-312-07031-4
    1. Generative organs, Male. 2. Andrology—Popular works. I. Title.
QP253.P87 1992   612.6'1—dc20   91-38693

First Edition: April 1992

10 9 8 7 6 5 4 3 2 1

CONTENTS

INTRODUCTION

*Poor little men! Poor little strutting peacocks! They spread
out their tails as conquerors almost as soon as they are able to
walk.*

—JEAN ANOUILH FROM *CeCile*, 1949

In order to understand the workings of the male mind, it's best
to start at the bottom and work upward. Ignorance about
the male body has unjustly given rise to a number of fallacies, maliciously spread around by the fair sex. That the
way to a man's heart is through his stomach has never been
confirmed by any anatomical studies. None of today's advanced explorative techniques have verified that two thirds
of a man's brain mass is located below his belt. And the
rumor that the remaining third shares a remarkable similarity to that found in the higher apes appears from recent
research to be only partly true.

But men themselves should take the main portion of
blame for this ignorance. For thousands of years, man has
kept his private parts too private. When Soranus two thousand years ago wrote the first textbook of gynecology, the
branch of medicine dealing with female complaints and dis-

eases, nobody said "But what about male diseases?" Maybe the ancient Roman men never had any problems in that department, or maybe they didn't like admitting they were a little less than perfect.

Even today, men usually have to be dragged screaming to the doctors if something is wrong with their sexual equipment. For some, the journey is made only after repeated threats of starvation from their fed-up partners. The shroud of secrecy that surrounds the workings and structure of the male organs smells of a male conspiracy with long roots. After all, if a man's sexual machinery was not oiled and in top working order, he not only risked being kicked out of his local and exclusive male club, but also could suffer a large dent in his smooth image as far as the ladies were concerned. Take, for example, the skillful way men have avoided the burden of birth control. It is said that if there had been more women working in contraceptive research, we would have had an effective male pill twenty years ago. In addition, we know far more today about why some women can't become pregnant than we do about the causes of infertility in men. It has only been in the last few years that men have had to admit to themselves and the rest of the world that they can have all sorts of problems with their internal sex organs, something that women have been complaining loudly about for hundreds of years.

The cracks in this shell of secrecy begin to appear in the 1950s with the rise in feminism and the birth of the so-called permissive society. Women began to demand orgasms and to put the male's sexual performance under a microscope. They read letters in women's magazines about the sexual lives of other women and compared notes. The bluff that men had practiced so expertly for a thousand years was suddenly called. Words of derision like "macho male" and "chauvinistic pig" appeared, as women for the first time dared to sneer at the animal within their mates. As cracks become chasms, men gradually become imperfect both to themselves and to the growing multitudes of interested female spectators. The myths and the stereotyped images have been cast aside, and the time has come for both women and men to discover the truth about maleness and find out what makes men tick.

Women have been going to gynecologists for decades, keeping a stiff upper lip and holding desperately to the shreds of their dignity as their sexual organs were inspected by doctors and hordes of medical students. Few men have suffered the indignity of spreading their legs and having their genitals closely scrutinized under bright lights by a member of the opposite sex. Not so long ago, a report appeared in the national press about an elderly gentleman who had suffered the indescribable embarrassment of being exposed to a group of medical students while in an undignified position during a urological examination. The worst was that among the crowd were female students "old enough to be his granddaughter." Women from all over the land must have had a hard time suppressing knowing grins and the odd fit of delirious laughter. It's certainly true that a man standing with his trousers and underwear around his socks awaiting the doctor's examination is not the same magnificent proud male we see in the human zoo.

It's not enough for a woman to live with a man to know him. To really understand this strange creature, his frustrations, his idiosyncrasies and peccadillos, she needs to take a university course, and earn a diploma in maleness—theory and practice. Maybe even dissect the odd male corpse or two to see how he really looks beneath his macho shell. Men will surely benefit from such a process of education. A man may acquire an ally, earn long-awaited sympathy from an increasingly suspicious and cynical partner, and perhaps even be released from the unbearable pressure of acting out the male role. This book constitutes an introduction to andrology, the science of men, for both women and men—a magical mystery tour around the male sexual organs in health and disease. It will be, I hope, a lasting contribution to peace and understanding between the sexes.

MAN'S

PROUDEST

PARTS

1

THE TESTICLES,

ORGANS

OF TRUTH

Most men know where they'd be without their testicles—in the land of hairless chins and falsetto voices. Without these little hormone generators, Rambo would be walking around in high heels and sporting a twenty-four-inch cup. Even though the organ in the middle is usually in the spotlight and often steals the show, it's the twin impresarios in the wings that manage the evening's performance and put the traveling male circus on the road. Within them lies the very secret of maleness: the source of testosterone, the male hormone. But the size of our testicles tells us little about how much male hormone they discharge into the blood. Most of the space inside them is occupied by yards of micro-thin tubing, like balls of wool, containing the sperm factories. Like car production lines, they gradually transform ordinary-looking cells into millions upon millions of sleek mini Ferraris, their motors warmed up and ready to go. The hormone factories lie discretely in small islands between the tubes, only a small percent of the testicles' total volume. It's an interesting thought that someone like Arnold Schwarzenegger could have testicles the size of chick peas and still be able to tear telephone directories in two.

Normally, testicles are the size of pigeon's eggs—about one and three quarters to two inches long and one inch wide—and in most cases the left hangs lower and is a bit smaller than the right. Some have suggested that nature has dangled them at different levels to keep them from painfully pressing against each other when we put our legs together or cross our knees. Differences in testicle size from species to species appear to be related to the demands that are placed on them to produce sperm and are largely due to differences in the number and length of the sperm factory tubing. If we compare the equipment of various apes, including ourselves, the variation in testicle size compared to body weights is spectacular, almost fifteenfold. The chimpanzee sports the largest with an organ 0.269 percent of its body weight, man comes in a poor second with 0.079 percent, while the gorilla has a mini 0.018 percent. In contrast, the size of the ovaries of the different apes is remarkably similar. These differences in testis size seem to correlate with how sexually active the animals are in the wild state and not with how much male hormone circulates in their bodies.

Within our own and other species size can be a hereditary factor; if the father was well equipped there's a good chance that the son is also. In China, the average weight of the right testicle is 10 grams; for a European the average is closer to 22 grams. Although this may be partly related to differences in body size, it's also likely to reflect genetic differences among the races. After all, if bulls can be selected for their testicle size by careful breeding, why not *Homo sapiens*?

And while we're still on the subject of testicular size, fertility doctors can often predict how many millions of sperm a man produces by a glance at the size of his testicles. In fact, anything damaging the delicate sperm tubes, such as infection, injury, or radiation, will have major effects on the size of the testicles. One of the side effects of anabolic steroids, the synthetic male hormone whose abuse is so often publicized in the mass media, is that they can make a man "small down there." This is because the drug fools the brain into switching off the hormones that control sperm production, laying off the sperm factories, and causing the testicles to shrink.

THE PAINFUL REALIZATION

Small boys first become aware of their testicles when they get kicked in them. It seems to be nature's way of reminding them that they have something very important between their legs that deserves special protection during the coming years. Most men cry "Shame!" when they hear that little old ladies in self-defense courses are taught to "Kick 'em in the balls, deary, they don't like that you know." And if you have ever seen a row of soccer players standing between the goal and a penalty kick, you soon see which of their bodily organs are given the highest priority—and it's not their eyes!

> Two young boys were tearing down the road on a trolly with a dog tied to the front when a policeman stepped out and flagged them down.
>
> "That's very cruel," he said, as he bent down to cut the string. But then he noticed a second string tied around the dog's testicles. "My goodness," he said, cutting the second string, "this gets worse!"
>
> At this point the front boy turns to his mate. "Shit, there goes our overdrive."

ORGANS OF TRUTH

Our ancestors appear to have held their testicles in very high esteem, not only because they were the very root of maleness but also because they contained the source of generations to come—a guarantee of preserving the family line. In Biblical lands, taking an oath was a serious business and to indicate your sincerity you put your hand on the testicles of the man to whom the promise was made. It is believed that by doing this, you accepted the implied threat that the unborn generations, those yet to spring from his genitals, would seek revenge if you broke your word or told a lie. Words such as "testify," "testimonial," and "testament" all originate from this association between truth and the testicles. Today, testifying in court involves raising your right hand in the air instead of sticking it under the judge's robes. And it's much easier writing down a testament than sealing it by putting your hands down the trousers of all your relatives. The Bible is full of accounts of people swearing on their "stones," a word that in modern editions has been replaced by tamer words such as "loins" or "thighs." In ancient Hebrew, a man's descendants were those who came out of his thigh.

> And Abraham said unto his eldest servant of his house, that ruled over all that he had "Put I pray thee, thy hand under my thigh: And I will make thee swear by the Lord, the God of heaven, and the God of the earth, that thou shall not take a wife unto my son of the daughters of the Kanaanites, among whom I dwell" (Genesis 24:1–3).

In those days, men unlucky enough to belong to the ESS (Empty Scrotum Society) weren't exactly respected members of society. In Roman times they couldn't testify in court. Going to church was also out of the question because according to the Law of Moses:

> He that is wounded in the stones or hath his privy member cut off shall not enter the congregation of the Lord (Deuteronomy 23:1).

Even in Israel today, men who have lost their testicles cannot marry naturally born Jewish woman. Instead they must make do with women who have been converted to Judaism or who have been born out of marriage.

One condition for getting married or for becoming a priest in the Roman Catholic church was the possession of a pair of balls. Roman Catholics may never forget the time when by mistake they elected a woman, Johanna, as pope. To make sure that this never happened again, the cardinals voting in a new pope were required to be 100 percent certain that the bulge under the vestments were the real articles. A special marble throne with a strategically placed hole was made through which the pope's sex organs could be felt by one of the cardinals. The priest then announced to the audience after touching the pope-to-be's private parts *"Testiculos habet et bene pedentes,"* which very roughly translated meant "Relax, guys, it's all there." The members of the Sacred College then celebrated the virility of the new pope by singing words to the effect "For he's a jolly good fellow!" It's not clear what the cardinal would have said and what the bishops would have sung if groping fingers had felt organs of the opposite sex!

With all these and the more obvious drawbacks, it's not surprising that men preferred to hold on to their testicles at all costs, and, in many lands, laws were written to help man do just that. It seems that in olden days women had a reputation as dirty fighters with a tendency to reach for a man's testicles in the heat of an argument. In the Old Testament it's written that:

> When men fight with one another, and the wife of the one draws near to rescue her husband from the hand of him who is beating him and puts her hand and seizes him by the private parts, then you shall cut off her hand (Deuteronomy 25:11–12).

Meanwhile in ancient Assyria . . .

> If a woman has crushed a man's testicle in an affray, one of her fingers shall be cut off, and if, although a physician has bound it up, the second

testicle is inflamed or, if she has crushed the second testicle in the affray, both her breasts or nipples shall be torn off.

On the other hand, according to Assyrian laws there were situations when even your testicles were not immune: If a husband caught his wife in bed with another man, he was at liberty to kill them both or cut off his wife's nose and castrate the man.

An irate man with a shotgun bursts in on his unfaithful wife in bed with her lover. He gets the man out of bed and threatens to shoot his testicles off. The lover suddenly falls on his knees and begs "No, please, I'm sorry, please give me a chance." "OK," the husband replies calmly, "start them swinging."

THE KEEPERS OF THE BED

Eunuch, the word we use for men without testicles, comes from the Greek, meaning "keepers of the bed." It recalls the times when sultans, kings, and princes had armies of wives and harems and needed somebody they could trust to keep them in order. We all have mental pictures of the eunuch—a large, fat, sluggish guy waving a palm-leaf fan in a Turkish harem, surrounded by sexual temptation to which he was unable to yield. In fact, their appearance depended on when they were castrated. If they lost their credentials long before puberty they became tall and thin. This is because there was no male hormone to put the brakes on the growth of the long bones in their arms and legs—something that normally takes place toward the end of puberty. Removing the testicles after puberty gave them the appearance of neutered tomcats—fat and cuddly.

The Persians were believed to be the first to castrate men

for this specific purpose, and long after the practice spread eastward to China where it became an industry. In ancient China eunuchs were originally supposed to manage the affairs of the harem, but they often rose to positions of trust and respect, becoming military commanders, administrators, and advisors. Because they had lost many of their male characteristics and virility, their nature was often arrogant, cruel, and suspicious—admirable qualities for a high-ranking soldier. They were outsiders in society and often became obsessed with power and wealth as compensation for their lost maleness, and because of their bitterness and hate for their fellow men, they often made the best torturers and executioners. It makes you wonder about the scrotal contents of some of today's successful businessmen and even more about some of today's heads of state.

A man who was having an affair with a Chinese man's wife was stopped by her husband one day who beat him up and warned him that if he continued to see his wife he would invoke the curse of the three Chinese tortures. The seducer just laughed and planned to visit the man's wife again the same night. The following morning the playboy woke up in his first-floor bedroom with a terrible pain in his chest. When he opened his eyes there was a huge rock atop his chest that made his breathing more and more difficult. On the rock was printed "Chinese torture #1." He laughed and since he was a strong man, simply lifted the rock and threw it out the window. Just after he let go the rock turned and he saw printed underneath a second sign that read "Chinese torture #2—right testicle attached to rock." The man, who was quick-witted, dived out of the window after the rock. As he dived over the windowsill he saw a third sign "Chinese torture #3—left testicle tied to leg of bed.

Castration usually took place before puberty. Prisoners of war usually lost only their testicles, which was assumed to pacify and humiliate them. The testicles were either burned with red hot irons or bound with tight cord, which, after a short time, made them wither and fall off. The Romans devised a special castration clamp with a hole through which the penis was inserted. The testicles were squeezed in the jaws of the clamp and a sharp knife did the rest. Eunuchs destined for the harems or the king's court usually lost both their penises and testicles with a clean sweep of a curved blade. This was probably because it was known that castration did not always eliminate sexual desire and men could get an erection for some time afterward depending at what age the testicles were removed. Both their thighs and abdomens were tightly wrapped in bandages to reduce bleeding before the operation. For three days they were not allowed to drink water after which a metal or bamboo tube was pushed up into the bladder to allow them to urinate. In most cases, they had no control over their urination and had to use diapers. The result was everybody knew when a eunuch was in the neighborhood, especially if you were downwind. Many young men suffered a miserable death from infection following the castration. Those who survived reverently placed their testicles in spirit until such time as the three of them could be buried together.

Later in China, eunuchs were given permission to marry. Much was written not only by the eunuchs themselves but also by their wives about the extreme sexual frustration of seeing naked concubines that they were unable to touch. Their wives wrote of their husbands' tormented fury as they attempted orgasm during conjugal sex. One of these eunuchs, a high-ranking official called Li, attempted to satisfy his lusts by strapping himself to young men so that the lower part of their bodies became substitutes for his own, which was said to move "with the full fury of a raging lion." Eunuchs desperately tried to regain their sexuality, resorting to magic, strange concoctions, and aphrodisiacs—in an attempt to make their genitals grow again. High on the menu was semen, menstrual blood, human placenta, and fresh human brains. Some emperors must have believed in these remedies because there are several accounts of them ordering their eunuchs to submit to a second shave when they suspected that their organs had begun to grow back again.

THE ULTIMATE SACRIFICE

The word castration, meaning the act of removing the testicles, is traditionally believed to come from the Latin word for beaver, *castor*. This wily animal, when attacked, was believed to chew off and leave behind its own testicles to give its predator something to think about while it made its getaway. The Romans made up the word *castorare*, meaning to act like the beaver and chew someone's balls off.

Although most eunuchs had the job done for them, there have been many groups of religious fanatics who gladly did the job themselves. Today if a man were asked to sacrifice something precious to prove his devotion to his god, he might offer a television or video recorder. In ancient times, the first thing that came to mind was his testicles. In fact, history is full of religious fanatics, such as the followers of the goddess Cybele, who felt that sacrificing one's sex life didn't go far enough to prove devotion and humility. They also hacked off their private parts to stress the point and then ran through the streets, throwing them through the nearest windows.

This irresistible urge to sacrifice a testicle or two to our maker has been around for a long time. Thankfully, many cultures got around the problem by coming to a compromise with their gods. Circumcision, according to the Jews, is "the uneffaceable mark of the contract between man and God." In fact, this form of symbolic castration has been around since the Iron Age and even mummies have been found without foreskins. The last fanatical sect to sacrifice their balls in large numbers were the followers of Skoptsi, who practiced their strange beliefs in Russia from the mid-1800s up to the start of the twentieth century. It was André Ivenov who woke up one day, came to the conclusion that there was too much sex in society, and then promptly castrated himself. Being an unselfish man and not wanting to keep this idea to himself, he persuaded a couple of thousand others to follow suit. In fact, just before the Russian Revolution the sect could boast 100,000 members of both sexes. After two children, the marriage was officially declared over and the men sacrificed their testicles, the women their clitorises. In the local societies, members of the sect were highly respected and often became prominent members because of their integrity and abstinence from all "sins of the flesh."

In 1950, several scientific articles advocated castration as a remedy for sex crimes. The male hormone had been isolated a little more than a decade earlier and people were just getting used to the remarkable way it could influence sexual behavior. In one institution, "experiments" on its inmates showed conclusively that after castration, sexual perverts and rapists changed their behavior patterns. When they were then given injections of male hormone the inmates became deviants again. The message was clear, and in San Diego, California, between 1955 and 1975, 397 sex offenders chose to lose their balls rather than serve long jail sentences. Between 1929 and 1959 in Denmark, which must have been ahead of its time, 300 prisoners made the same choice. In Britain and Germany, chemical castration was preferred, using drugs that neutralized the effects of the male hormone. The problem was making sure that the prisoners kept their word and took their medicine regularly!

FALSETTO

Although the Christian church was one of the first to denounce castration, it was also responsible for the revival of the practice in the sixteenth century—for a strange reason. Singing for God was a noble task, but the tones had to be pure and angelic and, preferably, at least at that time, not belong to the fair sex. Prepubescent boys were the logical choice and with the aid of a little snip here and there to encourage lengthening of the vocal cords, their falsetto voices could be perpetuated. Italian parents eagerly subjected their sons to the castrator's knife to preserve their precious soprano voices for the glory of God and at the same time guarantee a seat in the great choir in the sky. They became known as Castrati, and France established eunuch factories to keep up with the demand, sending them all over Europe. The most famous of them were worshiped like pop stars, and great composers even wrote special pieces for them. It wasn't until 1770 that a pope banned the practice and put an end to the industry once and for all.

A man on holiday in Spain visits a restaurant near the local bull ring. He can't speak Spanish but notices the man next to him being served an extraordinary but tasty looking dish: two large beefy filets smothered in onions and a creamy sauce. "I'd like that," he says, pointing to the neighbor's meal. "I'm sorry, Señor," replied the waiter. "That is the house specialty and only one is prepared every day. But if you like, I will reserve tomorrow's portion for you. The bullfight is at three, so please come at four."

The next day at four the man is sitting at his table waiting for his meal. The waiter comes with two little dried up nuggets smothered in onions and sauce and the man becomes furious. "That's not the same dish you served yesterday. Where are the juicy filets?" "A thousand pardons, Señor, but sometimes the bull wins!"

Our testicles are our passport to manhood and the visible evidence of maleness. Elderly men who have lost their testicles as part of the treatment for prostate cancer often jump at the chance of having their empty scrotums filled with artificial substitutes. Some even argue about the size. And why not? Their function may have all but ceased a decade before but their symbolic significance goes far deeper and persists. After all, was it not their testicles that gave them an identity, shaped their behavior, gave meaning to life—organs of dignity and truth?

2 THE PHALLIC CONNECTION

In our world nothing is so esteemed in a man as a good weighty zabb just as a jutting backside is the most excellent thing in a woman.

—*Arabian Nights*

Most men (and a few very strange women) are in possession of a penis, and, just like other parts of the male body, they come in all shapes and sizes. "Penis psychology" gives us a fascinating insight into the human male and his primitive roots.

THE BIGGER THE BETTER?

When George Washington was asked how long should legs be, he replied "Long enough to reach the ground." Maybe he could have given a similar answer if the question had been "How long should a penis be?" Not that it should reach the ground, but, like legs, it should be long enough to do the job. A wise man once said that the only thing that most penises have in common is that they are the wrong size or shape as far as their owners are concerned.

Why do so many men go around thinking that they don't have the equipment to do the job properly? The answer is that from cradle to grave, men are exposed to a subtle form of brainwashing telling them that they have smaller equipment than everybody else. It starts rather innocently when little Peter, after several years of secretly mocking his sister's excuse for a penis, one day gets a peek at the monstrosity owned by his father. A glance at his naked little widdler and he already feels he's woefully inadequate.

Puberty arrives with its inevitable interest in girlie magazines and the odd soft-porn pictures. And just when he feels he is finally catching up to his father in the genital stakes, one look at those nude, male models romping around with their exposed dongs flapping impressively in the wind, and what could have been a penis becomes a widdler again. Rumors exist that even Elvis had to push a long piece of rubber tubing down his pants to earn more shrieks from the crowd for his pelvic gyrations. And then there are the showers at school. It's strange how the first to get wet are precocious mighty midgets with luxuriant growths of pubic hair and above-average penises.

Seeds of doubt remain dormant, watered during puberty, bursting to germinate—awaiting the big confrontation with a man's first sexual partner when the goods are finally on first approval. He waits for the magic words, "Oh my God, it's enormous!" or the dreaded silence followed by delirious laughter. The response may be more indirect . . .

A young man was walking in the park with his girlfriend and wondering whether he was properly equipped. He decides to test her by taking out his penis in the darkness and putting it in her hand. "No thank you, darling, you know I don't smoke!"

I guess he could have hoped that she thought it was a Cuban cigar!

It was a great relief for many men when certain books

and articles confirmed what they had been secretly hoping: that magazines such as *Playgirl* featured nude males that were apparently selected for the large size of their nonerect penises, about 50 to 100 percent over the national average. Not only that, since American magazines use mainly models with circumcised organs, it can be difficult to tell whether the penis is in a partially erect state.

Homosexuals also appear to be size worriers. A 1979 study of 1,000 gay men in the United States showed that although 37 percent thought that the penis size of a partner was very important, almost all admitted that they felt their own penis was too small.

AN APE WITH A BIG PENIS

When Desmond Morris said that men were apes with over-sized penises, more than half of the world's female population nodded their heads in agreement. Certainly our gorilla cousins don't have much to be happy about! An adult male gorilla tips the scales at nearly 600 pounds, about the weight of three good-sized men, but has an erection of about two inches. But then again, who laughs at a 600-pound gorilla? Desmond Morris feels that the reason why we have such big penises compared to the other apes is because we use it not only to deposit sperm in the vagina but also to give pleasure, an important way of cementing the human bond. He believes it was the increase in penis width that we evolved (which increased the friction on the vaginal walls) that made us so popular among the fair sex. Certainly, several studies have indicated that when given a choice, female monkeys and baboons often pick the male with the biggest organ and with the most staying power.

GETTING THE FACTS RIGHT

From the early 1900s, little men in white coats with rulers in their pockets have traveled to all corners of the world to answer such burning questions as, "Why do they make condoms in three sizes?" "Is it true what they say about Jamaicans?" and of course, "What about pygmies?" Let us start with your average warm-blooded Caucasian male. *The Atlas of Human Sex Anatomy*, a standard work in medical schools, puts the normal range of a soft penis roughly between 3 and 4 inches (circumference 2.5 to 4 inches) with an average length of 3.7 inches, data that is generally agreed upon by the experts. And here is an important point: be sure about the correct units. An Englishman could go into a deep depression by mixing up his inches with his centimeters.

Normally the erection adds about 50 to 60 percent to the length, so that Mr. Average will sport an erect organ around 6 inches varying between 4.7 and 7 inches, 3.1 to 4.7 inches in circumference. Kinsey showed that only 24 percent of men have penises of the "average" size. Only 5 percent of men have an erection less than 3.5 inches, and only one in a hundred is heavily armed with an erection greater than 9 inches. The length of the penis is usually worked out by measuring from the base on the overside to the tip. The size of the erect penis is calculated by first stretching the soft organ until a resistance is felt and then measuring once again from base to tip. Attempts at cheating by stretching the organ using mechanical assistance are not recommended!

Within each culture there appear to be at least two types of male organ. One is relatively small in the nonerect state (like a dried prune with all of its biological fluids squeezed out of it) because of the overactivity of certain nerves (the same ones that can make the penis shrink when subjected to a cold shower). When this organ becomes erect it can come as a pleasant surprise for an unsuspecting partner, transforming from a toothpick to a veritable flag pole. The other type is a bluffer. Partly filled with blood at all times, it can attract admiring glances from men in the showers and women in the bedroom, but when it comes to getting it erect, it can be a disappointment (at least for those women who are penis-fixed), adding relatively little to its final length. Masters and Johnson made a major point of the fact that there is relatively little variation among men in the size of their erect organs. They illustrate this point by describing two men, one who had a 3-inch soft penis that, when erect, was 6.5 inches, a difference of 120 percent. Another had a starting size of 4.3 inches that added only an extra 2.2 inches when erect, an increase of 50 percent.

IT IS TRUE WHAT THEY SAY ABOUT. . . ?

Dr. Jacobus was the pen name of a surgeon in the French military service who spent a lot of his time examining and measuring hundreds of male and female sex organs from Malaya to Africa. He published his results in 1935. According to Jacobus it was the African Negro, especially the Sudanese Negro, who was first in line when penises were given out to the human race. He described them as "stallion men," and other organ watchers like Sir Richard Burton, the famous explorer, agreed. The average size of the organ when limp was 5 to 5¾ inches; when erect, 7½ to 8 inches. The interesting thing was that "even when in complete erection it is still soft like that of a donkey and when pressed by the hand feels like thick india-rubber tube full of liquid." In contrast to the Negro, Hindu men appeared to have got "the short end of the deal" with a soft-organ size of a couple of inches transforming to an average erection of 4 to 4.5 inches. The good doctor was also impressed at the great difference in penis size between the African and Asian Arab. Whereas the pure-blooded Arabian Arab had a European-type penis, his African cousin could boast an erect organ of the long, thick, and flabby kind, around 7 inches. Although Egyptians are commonly thought of as Arabs, they have a penis that reveals their African roots.

But what about other races? Contrary to popular belief, French and Italian men don't appear to have better equipment than the rest. In the penis Olympics, after the African Negro in descending order is the European organ followed by the Japanese with a specimen 5 inches long. The Chinese male is on average about 1 inch longer and slightly thicker than the Japanese male. Jacobus and several other ethnologists made an important observation: the size of the penis closely follows the dimensions of the sex organs of the females of the same race, in particular the width of the vagina. Jacobus wrote: "It is certain that the Hindu women, whose men have small and slender penises, find that a normally constituted European is a trouble to them and suffer martyrdom when they have to do with a Negro or an Arab, whose enormously large penis is for them an instrument of torture." It seems that nature has a way of making members of the same race "stick together!"

PUT A KNOT IN IT

In the scientific and popular literature there seems to be a competition to see who can report the largest human penis. Doctors Kinsey, Jacobus, and Reuben's contributions vary around 9.5 to 14 inches. And there are celebrities who never get included in the official charts. John Holmes, probably one of the most famous porn stars of the motion picture industry and who recently died of AIDS, had a penis as long as the male forearm (14 inches) and about the same thickness. Even this record has now been surpassed by other film stars such as Moby Dick and Long Dong Silver, who can boast an incredible 18 inches and who are often shown in publicity photographs with a knot in it! Clearly when you have 200 million men in the world you will always find those "a shade out of the ordinary." The question is why are these freaks so popular. Certainly for many of the real heavyweights, sex is out of the question. Perhaps their popularity reveals a form of masochism that strengthens our own size conflicts, or perhaps it provides a deep form of sadism watching the female being impaled.

Seargent major to a soldier on the parade ground: "Private Hoskins, why is your penis hanging down below your shorts?"
  Private: "Cos it's cold and it's shrunk, sir!"

Why do flashers flash? Is it because they have monstrous organs with which they can terrify little old ladies? The answer is no. According to Kinsey, convicted flashers have average-sized organs, so they obviously flash for other reasons. Kinsey also studied the penis size of convicted rapists to see if they had anything special in the genital department. Once again the answer was no. In fact some of the most infamous rapist/murderers had very little to crow about. Dewitt Clinton Cook, an infamous rapist/murderer, had an organ in the amateur leagues, and one of the things that convicted the English rapist/murderer Harry Maclean was his small penis, which many of the women surviving his attacks remembered in vivid detail.

WHO CARES?

Before men start throwing themselves off cliffs like lemmings because of their "undersized" penises, it's a good idea to first ask their partners whether they give a damn about a couple of inches here and there! When Shere Hite asked women about sex, there was no spontaneous mention that they felt penis size was important, indicating that is not the first thing that came into their minds. In a similar survey by Zilbergeld in 1978 of 426 women, not one mentioned penis size as important. And we must not forget Masters and Johnson when they reminded us that it is the first one-third of the vagina that is the most responsive, well within reach of even Tiny Tim.

On the other hand, at least one female researcher went on record in 1978 saying that all this talk about the size of the penis being unimportant is a myth invented by men!

Keller interviewed fifty-seven sexually experienced women of whom 87 percent sang in chorus the bigger the better! For them the larger penis was aesthetically more beautiful and arousing and they enjoyed the feeling of being filled. Certainly this fits in with Desmond Morris's view that thickness separates us from our hairy cousins and converted the penis into an instrument of pleasure. But then again, the human vagina, according to learned men, displays an amazing ability to distend and shrink to accommodate all penis sizes and thus provide similar degrees of friction. In this great and confusing penis debate, maybe it's time that men began to be a little more selfish. . . .

A man undresses in front of his recently acquired girlfriend and unashamedly reveals his undersized penis. "Who do you think you are going to satisfy with that little thing?" she asks. "Me," he replies with a smile.

Is all this talk about penis size all in the woman's mind? Is it the imagined size that is so sexually stimulating? In one study in which men and women were allowed to read passages describing a sex scene between a man and a woman, the only thing that was changed was the size of the hero's penis, which varied from 3 to 5 to 8 inches. Afterwards the readers were asked to judge how arousing the passage was and why. The results indicated that the size of the imagined penis had no effect on the degree of arousal and their image of the man as a good or bad lover.

ONCE UPON A TIME . . .

As you would expect, the size of the penis is very dependent on the male hormone testosterone. In the first twelve to fourteen weeks of our uterine lives, the amount of testosterone we produce is determined by our mother's hormones. From then on we are on our own and we create these hormones ourselves. If the level of male hormone is not high enough in the first twelve to fourteen weeks, the sex organs don't develop properly and can resemble something halfway between the two sexes. If something happens to the levels later than fourteen weeks, the penis looks normal but can be a miniature version of the real thing. Pregnant women taking sex hormones to prevent a threatened abortion can risk disturbing the growth of their child's penis. From ten weeks, the penis gradually increases in size by around .03 inches a week, growing from .01 inch to a stretched size of 1½ inches at birth.

At ten years, it can be stretched to 2¼ inches and doubles at sixteen years as we go through puberty, once again because of the effects of a surge of testosterone in the blood. It's also assumed that growth hormone is necessary for penis growth because dwarfs who lack this hormone also have penises in proportion to their height, even when there is sufficient male hormone around. As with the development of every other organ and system in our bodies, the normal development of our sex organs depends on a precisely timed, highly complex system with many steps, any one of which can fail, turning us from a Long Dong Silver into a General Tom Thumb.

If a boy is born with a very small penis (often called a micropenis) due to not having enough male hormone, it can be encouraged to grow again either by injecting the hormone or by simply rubbing some hormone cream on it regularly. What is interesting is that this treatment appears to increase the number of cells in the penis and even if the treatment then stops, the organ stays around the same size. This explains why if you castrate an adult, his sex organ stays about the same size even though it's of about as much use as a front zipper on women's trousers. It is strange to think that if our mothers had rubbed a little bit of the appropriate cream on the right place at the right time, the world would be filled with John Holmeses and a lot of very nervous women.

Sadly, once puberty is passed, the fate of our sexual organs is sealed and we have to live with the number of cells God gave us. To date there is no magic hormone that we can use to increase the growth of our penis once puberty is passed. Sure, we can transplant lumps of muscle on the end like the Japanese do, we can make it swell by rubbing it with the bristles of certain insects as practiced by certain native tribes, and we can fill it to a maximum with blood using handy vacuum pumps, but no matter how much we stretch it, play with it, or plead with it, we cannot increase the number of its cells and therefore have a hard job changing its size.

DEAR DOCTOR RUTH

Some of those men who are insecure about the size of their penis, after years of keeping it hidden from their fellow man, after years of pushing socks down their trousers, finally pluck up the courage to mention their worries to their own doctors or in desperate situations even write to somebody like Dr. Ruth. Usually the move is not regretted. Often a man may contact the doctor for an entirely different reason—an ingrown toenail, for example. But gradually the ingrown toenail, by some miracle of verbal contortion, turns into an ingrown penis. The first thing the doctor has to do is to exclude the rare possibility that his patient has some hormone disturbance or a chromosome problem. After that's done, the question is usually raised about what is normal. Some doctors illustrate the point by showing a series of rubber penis models that represent the normal range, from the economy size to the super deluxe. From these, the "patient" can often understand that he has overestimated what is normal and may even leave the room feeling a few inches prouder.

It's always a good idea to remember the six basic laws of genital physics: (1) The smaller the penis, the proportionally greater the erection. (2) Friction in the first 1 to 1½ inches of the vagina is what counts. (3) The human vagina adapts to all penises. (4) Thickness is better than length. (5) It's not what you've got, its the way that you use it. And (6) there is always somebody worse off than yourself. With these basics firmly implanted in his mind our man should now be ready once again to take his place in human society.

But there are always those who scornfully cast aside these pearls of wisdom as lies and propaganda. They come for practical advice, and it's practical advice the doctors have to give. The Japanese have a saying, "A faithful wife has no knowledge of big and little penises." In other words, one way of avoiding the problem is to marry a virgin. On the other hand, a charming story from the Middle Ages indicates that this is not always so simple:

> A man with a small penis suspects his new wife of previously having many lovers and decides to trap her. Exposing his penis to her on their wedding night, he asks, "Do you think you could endure such a big one, my Love?" Cleverly understanding the plan, the wife innocently replies, "My dearest husband, how could I possibly know if it is a big one or whether I could contain it?" She got away with it that time.

Another piece of advice is that our size worrier should perfect other techniques of making love—try to compensate for his missing inches by being an expert in sensuous massage, in oral sex, in the art of ear titillation, or by simply being a considerate lover. Remember the old saying, "It's no good being built like a bull if all you can do is charge like one!" Some sexologists advise the man with the small penis to penetrate his partner early in the excitement phase, before her vagina has fully expanded, so that the friction is more intense.

In India, Vatsyayana's sex manual, *Kamasutra*, which was written in 400 A.D., made a major issue of sexual sizes. A man was a hare man, a bull man, or a horse man depending on the size of his penis or lingam. A woman was a deer, mare, or cow-elephant depending on the size of her vagina or yoni. The idea was that a hare man should restrict his sex life to deer women and was advised against having sex with the large herbivores. The idea is not a bad one; the problem for the hare man is plucking up enough courage to date enough women to find the right fit. Other possibilities are wearing rubber penis extenders, using vacuum pumps that have supposedly been shown scientifically to increase the swelling power of the spongy tissue of the penis, and to try new sexual positions that can help increase the friction between the two organs.

GOING ROUND THE BEND

Having a penis of the right size is one thing, but if it is shaped like a boomerang it can make intercourse a painful experience for both partners. Two words that should strike fear into all men with straight penises are Peyronie's disease, named after the Frenchman who first described it. On one side of the penis a fibrous area develops that gradually contracts, drawing the penis to the same side. Another condition that can cause the penis to bend is a weakness in the fibrous sheath surrounding the spongy tissue. This time when the penis becomes erect it bends away from the weak side. Both of these problems can cause intense pain and make a man celibate, but surgery can often correct the problem.

Some unfortunate men are born with their sex organs switched around, that is, with their testicles above the penis instead of below it. Since there is no treatment for this condition the only advice is to have sex very carefully. Others are born with their organs growing out of other parts of their bodies, such as their thighs. The organs in this case are usually not functional in a reproductive sense, and are most often surgically removed. Perhaps the most impressive penis aberration is to be born with two. Jean Baptisto dos Santos, a Cuban, was such a man. He had two large and fully operative male organs, and it is written that he "was possessed of extraordinary animal passion, the sight of a female alone be-

A SARTORIAL TIDBIT

An interesting subject of debate is "on which side does the penis hang when in repose?" A scientific study recently published in a reputable medical journal suggests that in 75 percent of the cases, it points naturally to the left when the subject is in the horizontal position. This conclusion was reached after looking at the X-ray pictures of 120 men with broken hips in which the outline of the penis can be clearly seen. This is apparently old news, because tailors have for many years been allowing for this extra volume on the left by cutting slightly more material on that side when making made-to-measure trousers. It is said that it is for this reason that the flap of material covering the zipper or buttons on the trousers is always on the left.

What is more difficult to explain is why the penis of most men tends to the left. What is probable is that the penis is naturally hinged that way, rather like it is natural for the left testicle to hang lower than the right. That men with left-hanging penises have some unique advantage is unlikely, although right-handed men do find it easier to extract the organ when it's lying on the left during a visit to the urinal, than when it's sneaked over to the opposite side!

ing sufficient to excite him. He was said to use both penises, after finishing with one, continuing with the other."

The possession of the perfect penis has been the dream of many mortal men. It became the physical evidence of their ability as lovers and the key to earning respect and admiration not only from their female sexual partners but also from their male competitors. A primitive attitude it may be, but an inseparable feature of maleness will the penis always remain.

3 THE FORGOTTEN FORESKIN

In America alone this year, 1.3 million boys will sacrifice their foreskins to the surgeon's knife—½ inch of discarded penile anatomy. What is this thing which is treated with so much disdain by so many? Has the supreme being made a minor blunder in his blueprint for the male of the species?

WHAT IS THIS THING CALLED A FORESKIN?

The penis is not just a club to be used to batter its way through the portals of love. It is a wonder of natural hydraulic engineering equipped at its tip with a dense mat of nerve endings that make it one of the most sensitive organs in the male body, designed to fire off impulses to our pleasure center in the brain and spinal cord with the slightest touch. It is clear that such a delicate and sensitive piece of machinery should be protected from the ravages of nature and its local environment when not in use—a function provided by the humble foreskin. Whether it be on request or on its own initiative, this guardian of the male member gracefully slides back to expose its sensitive core, charged and ready for action. To call it a skin is to do it an injustice because it is far more. To remind us of its sexual significance it is equipped with an intricate biochemical apparatus that makes it responsible to the male sex hormone. Indeed human foreskins have been studied by hormone researchers for many years in an attempt to unlock some of the secrets of how the male hormone acts. It also contains highly specialized glands that squeeze out an oily substance on the penile head to prevent it from drying out and to hinder attack by bacteria and fungus. Some have suggested that this oil may also serve as a sexual perfume to attract and excite the female during sexual play. Let us not forget that women too have foreskins, small and well hidden but nevertheless fulfilling the function of its male equivalent.

FORESKIN ADORNMENT

When our more primitive tribal cousins discovered a loose or redundant piece of body skin, the chances were that they stretched it to unbelievable lengths, mutilated it, or pierced it with all manner of objects from chicken bones to rings. In this respect, the foreskin has through the ages apparently been a temptation too great to resist. Even in today's so-called civilized societies, body piercers, bondage freaks, and the more temperate masochists have been quick to appreciate the potential of their foreskins for adornment and for titillating their sex lives. A ring placed on one side of the foreskin is not only chic but also serves to heighten the woman's sexual pleasure during intercourse. Gay pairs in the United States have hit on a novel way of proving their sexual fidelity by putting padlocks through the foreskin and giving their partners the key.

Long pendulous foreskins are apparently a thing of beauty for some of the tribes in New Guinea who deliberately stretch them by suspending weights from the penis. Foreskin stretching may be something to recommend for the Chinese who are apparently equipped with relatively short foreskins, with the consequence that the naked head often peeps out even in the flaccid organ, giving the appearance of an acorn. The resemblance of the semierect penis to an acorn possibly accounts for the use of the oak tree in sexual symbolism.

THE RAPE OF THE PHALLUS

Man has slit, skewered, and hacked pieces of his penis skin since he first discovered it hanging there between his legs. How much skin he removed from it depended on the culture to which he belonged. Those boys unfortunate enough to belong to certain Arabian subcultures could look forward to having all the outer skin removed from their penis down to the base, and woe betide those who cried out during the ceremony; they were put to death by their fathers. Some races were satisfied with a symbolic nick in the foreskin, while others, such as the modern American culture, preferred to remove the whole end. Egyptian mummies have been found minus their foreskins, and some of the Indians who greeted Columbus when he discovered America were also circumcised.

Why? you may ask. In some cultures it appeared to represent an initiation ceremony at puberty. Boys could show how macho they were by smiling while their genitals were being mutilated. Experts have also pointed out that this ritual spilling of blood may also represent a symbolic menstruation—a sign of the happy times to come. Other societies had more religious reasons. As mentioned earlier, circumcision can be thought of as a symbolic castration that was the ultimate offering to the gods. In Genesis 17:10–14 it is written that God is said to have claimed as his covenant that every boy should be circumcised:

> And he that is eight days old shall be circumcised among you, every man-child in your generations, and the uncircumcised man-child, whose flesh of

his foreskin is not circumcised, that soul shall be cut off from his people: he hath broken my covenant.

In other words, one's foreskin was the membership fee for a rather exclusive religious club. In certain African and Melanesian tribes the operation is one of a variety of ritual mutilations that are performed in the hope of adding allure and charm to the penis.

So much for the original origins of circumcision. Why does the operation find so much favor in contemporary Western society? In the 1850s in America, the humble foreskin was blamed for a long list of disorders, from epilepsy to "reflex neuroses leading to idiocy." Mental illness was blamed on tight foreskins, so-called sphincterism, as was excessive masturbation. The foreskin was a disease-causing structure that had no business being there. These sentiments were still being published in medical textbooks as late as 1925. Today, aside from religious reasons, there are very few sound arguments for removing the foreskin. The majority of parents allow their sons' foreskins to fall under the surgeon's knife because (a) everybody else does it, (b) the fact that they look different from their fathers might create a psychological problem for some sons, (c) it is easier to keep a circumcised penis clean, (d) it is aesthetically nicer to look at, and (e) the doctor didn't say we shouldn't.

Until recently two "scientific" arguments were that uncircumcised men run a greater risk of getting cancer of the penis and that they also cause cancer of the cervix in women with whom they have had sex. The villain in the plot was supposed to be smegma, the cheesy substance that collects under the foreskin of the uncircumcised male. This theory is now rapidly losing support. The key today is penile hygiene, whether you are circumcised or not. It appears to be "in" to pamper your penis with the loving care it deserves. "If we can teach a boy to brush his teeth, clean his ears, and wipe his anus, would it be too much to teach him to retract his foreskin and wash the head of his penis?"

retorted one expert on the subject. A penis should be washed as often as you brush your teeth, but not necessarily only after meals and with a strong brush. Such a change in social attitudes would also remove another argument for circumcision—that it prevents the local buildup of fungus or bacteria under the foreskin that is responsible for the painful condition called balanitis and also removes a potential breeding ground for venereal disease.

What are the remaining grounds for circumcision? These include (a) a foreskin which is too tight and cannot be pulled back, (b) a condition called paraphimosis, in which the base of the foreskin is so tight that it strangles the blood flow to the penis head, (c) repeated inflammation or infection of the glans, (d) abnormalities of the foreskin after an accident, or (e) skin cancer of the penis. For the most part, however, these conditions are extremely rare.

THE GOOD NEWS AND THE BAD NEWS

The bad news starts from the day we say good-bye to our foreskins. Not only are there complications of the operation itself, such as bleeding and infection, but also our newly uncovered glans is now uncomfortably exposed to ammonia and other harmful chemicals from urine and feces, and suffers the abrading influence of toilet paper and clothing. The result can be painful sores and a condition called meatal stenosis, which is the hardening and narrowing of the urethral opening.

With loss of the foreskin the man loses a natural gliding mechanism that helps with the sex act. With a foreskin it is possible for the shaft to move back and forth within the loose outer skin. This is especially helpful during sex with women who have poor lubrication because the reduced friction during intercourse is less irritating. This is also the case with anal sex. Penetration by the circumcised man has been compared to thrusting the foot into a sock held open at the top, while penetration by his uncircumcised counterpart has been likened to slipping the foot into a sock that has been previously rolled up.

After circumcision, the delicate and sensitive skin of the head of the penis gradually changes character. After years of rubbing against underwear and denim jeans, it begins to resemble normal skin and loses some of its sensitivity, with a reduction in the intensity of sensations for the man during intercourse as a possible result.

Having sex with a circumcised penis has been likened to "trying to appreciate one of Goya's masterpieces by looking at a black and white photograph." The good news is that circumcision could help a man stay on the job longer, thus avoiding the disgrace of premature ejaculation. One additional piece of good news for the circumcised male is that he never has to suffer the painful experience of getting something stuck under a foreskin. British and Commonwealth soldiers who suffered the sandstorms of the African deserts in the last war were somewhat more comfortable than their uncircumcised brothers. Perhaps this is the reason why circumcision finds so much favor with Aborigines and Arabs of the desert regions in Australia and the Middle East.

If it is not yet obvious to the reader, the message is clear and undeniable: Our foreskin, like our tonsils, does have a purpose in life, and it is time that one-sixth of the world's population faced the reality of that fact. Happily, in America if new attitudes persist and current trends continue, the coming generation, unlike the previous one, can revel in the new experience of having sex with a foreskin.

4 BODY HAIR AND THE LION'S MANE

Although a pair of testicles is in most cases the only credentials needed for entering the male club, other signs of maleness, programed into our bodies millions of years ago, make the application for life membership go much more smoothly. The broad shoulders, the deep voice, the muscular arms, and of course all that hair sprouting from different crooks and crannies provide undeniable evidence that the male hormone, testosterone, has been at work, transforming, molding what could have been a ninety-eight-pound weakling into a macho machine.

Most of the function of our body hair was lost when monkeys started putting on trousers or wearing hats. But the special distribution of body hair in men has undoubtedly served an important function in our primitive past, signaling aggression to other men but also inviting sexual interest from the fair sex. And you can't erase overnight the significance of something that has taken millions of years to evolve. Deep within us, there are associations concerned with social and sexual displays. If the loss of head hair is a nightmare for women, a hairy upper lip or chest can be a disaster. Many men must have felt at some time the irresistible urge to strangle the odd waiter whose shirt is strategically opened to tell their female companions that his chest is hairier than their own.

It is not unreasonable to assume that body hair serves some sort of useful function. Hair, especially in the armpit and probably in the pubic area, has survived millions of years of evolution as a clever way of slowing down the release of sexy smells produced by special glands—our very own aerosol cans sending out puffs of male perfume with every body movement. Some have also suggested that they may also serve as cushions, reducing friction between skin areas that rub against each other during physical activity and sex. American women, with the enthusiastic support of men, today react nauseously or uncomfortably at least to a discussion about their armpit or leg hair. Most men would also keep their distance from men who bragged that they shaved their legs or their underarms.

But why are males hairier than the average female? Feminists might retort that it is clear evidence that men are at least three rungs lower on the evolutionary ladder. After all, the general evolutionary tendency for the human race is to shed their body hairs. Desmond Morris, author of *The Naked Ape*, is a great believer that one of the reasons why both sexes have become less hairy is so that skin sensitivity can be increased during erotic body contact. The hairless body has become not only a way of exaggerating the physical difference between the sexes, but also a female sexual signal designed to excite the hairier male through touch, which in turn reinforces her own sexual interest. Artists for centuries have exaggerated the smooth milky-white skin of their female nudes, an ideal that appears to be shared by the millions of women using tons of hair removal creams and electrical depilators every day.

FACIAL HAIR, THE LION'S MANE

It's difficult to imagine a use for the beard other than as some form of social or sexual signal. After all, many of our monkey relatives have some distinguishing color or bodily feature that makes them different from the rest of their ape cousins. It may be a long beard, hairy ears, bushy eyebrows, or some strange hairstyle. But the beard has also been described as the most intense masculine hair signal, equivalent to a lion's mane. Most believe it was probably more important in displays of aggression between rival males. A bushy untidy beard combined with long head hair would make the face seem larger than it really was and enhance the whiteness of the teeth when he told an opponent to push off. According to some experts that's why in today's "nonaggressive" society, most men shave off their beards, to switch off this provocative masculine signal. In the 1930s, a few sexologists dared to suggest that the "fashion" for clean-shaven men and women with boyish figures reflected tendencies to bisexuality in a decadent age. Today in the advertising business, in situations where a rugged, tough male needs to be portrayed, the choice is often an unshaven model with a five-o'clock shadow, a compromise between the beard and the pseudo-infantile image of the smooth face. The preference of certain women for bearded men may reflect a desire to be associated with partners who advertise their maleness in this way. Those preferring the smooth-chinned variety may more welcome the increased skin contact they can enjoy during sex. Recently, an American psychologist has suggested that when a mature man grows a beard, it may not only be to hide a double chin or demonstrate maturity, but it is the expression of an unconscious fear of losing his potency.

Some writers think that the male face has features that so resemble his sex organs that it may have evolved that way as a form of signaling . . . rather like the large breasts of the human female are supposed to remind the lustful male about the prize between her buttocks, and her fleshy lips are supposed to mimic her genital lips. Men have larger, more bulbous noses than women, and this could possibly remind a short-sighted female of his penis. The male nostrils are also more flared—attached to the nose like a mini pair of testicles? The point is that the hair on a man's face, like the eyebrows and beard, is bushier and coarser than head hair, more like pubic hair. When one of our female ancestors approached a male, the unconscious association between the nose in its bed of "pubic hair" and the sex organs would act as an attractor and make her come nearer for a closer look. A rival male would interpret it in the same way and run.

The beard has been looked upon since antiquity as a badge of virility and strength. The ancient Babylonians cherished it as a sign of manhood and the Hebrews thought of it not only as a sign of strength, but also as a mark of wisdom and seniority. In ancient Egypt, the beard was a sign of social rank, the unchallenged prerogative of all rulers. The upper classes often chose to wear artificial rather than real beards and their size told people to which rank they belonged. Even Queen Hatshepsut, a widow who reigned in Egypt from 1505 B.C., wore a false ceremonial beard to mark her authority. In Greece, there was the curious custom of touching a man's beard if you were seeking a favor, and in many cultures, especially up to the middle of the fifteenth century, cutting off a man's beard was one sure way of humiliating him.

SCALP HAIR

Both men and women would have very long hair if it was allowed to grow to its natural length. Scalp hair is therefore mainly a species signal. However, the hair on our heads is associated, albeit unconsciously, with sexual activity, and in many cultures, cutting if off symbolized castration, something that figures prominently in folk tales. When Delilah shaved off the seven locks of Samson's head, he lost his strength and virility. The awesome event of forcibly cutting off a man's hair or shaving his head was the final insult and a great indignity. Members of holy orders, Buddhists, Taoists, and Christians, often shaved their heads as outward signs of celibacy. The Friar Tuck hairstyle of European monks, with its crescent of hair surrounding a bald patch (the tonsure), was also a sign to the world that they were neutered and chaste. And as men grow old, they tend to lose their hair almost in synchrony with their virility—a valuable social signal fading with time.

Men can go bald for several reason, but the one that millions of men have in common is the dreaded "male pattern baldness." Balding men may try to fool their children for years with explanations for why they are becoming shiny on top. Being scalped by Indians is probably the hardest for kids to swallow. Frightened by ghosts is no better. And it doesn't help to provide them with a long list of famous heroes who were also bald, like Julius Caesar. They could of course try a super bluff and say that the majority of the male population including Rambo wears a wig. But, there comes a time when the truth has to be faced and little Henry has to be told that somewhere tucked away in his chromosomes are baldness genes. These genes work only if there is enough male hormone around. In fact, if little Henry had been castrated he could have taken a full head of hair with him to his grave. Eunuchs, who have no testicles and therefore little male hormone, do not become bald. If they've started to become a little bald before they are castrated, their hair pattern "freezes" and only begins to regress again with treatment with male hormone. So becoming bald depends on three things: age; baldness genes; and male hormone. Because eunuchs never lost their hair, the myth started that bald men produced buckets of male hormone and were exceptionally virile. In fact this is probably one of the great topics of conversation when men who are thin on top get together. When a famous celebrity was asked if he felt baldness improved sexual potency he replied, "Possibly, but it gives a man fewer chances of proving it." Although one scientific report (presumably by bald-headed authors) has shown that bald men do have higher levels of male hormone in their blood, the majority believe that just normal levels are necessary for the bald genes to work.

TESTOSTERONE AND THE SKIN

Our skin is a mirror of how much male hormone is circulating in the blood of both men and women. Skin that is influenced by the male hormone is thicker, oilier, hairier, and produces more sweat than skin bathed in the female sex hormones. The spotty face of puberty is evidence of the turmoil in the skin as testosterone is poured from the testicles into the blood. And any hormonal imbalance in women resulting in too much male hormone is soon reflected in the skin: elderly women with moustaches are simply telling the world that their ovaries have closed shop and their adrenals, which produce small amounts of male hormone, are now taking over the hormone business.

For a cell, tissue, or organ to react to the male hormone, it has to have the right lock into which the male hormone key can fit. These locks are called receptors and it's a clever way of making sure that one hormone can influence widely different organs spread out over the whole body. Other hormones are keys to different locks. Skin and other tissues such as muscles and the sex organs contain the same locks, so that when puberty starts, all of these doors are opened to the effects of the male hormone at the same time.

A strange quirk of nature is that, on rare occasions, there are men born without these testosterone receptors, with the result that none of the cells in their bodies can be turned into the male mode. Although they produce enough of the male hormone, their appearance resembles that of a female, with breasts and a short vagina. Their skin is smooth and except for the hair on their heads, there is a complete absence of body hair—no beards, no pubic hairs, no tufts of hair in their noses or ears, and they never get acne! These "men" tell us that it is the male hormone that is responsible for hair growth in both sexes.

But the situation is a little more complicated. Although it is the male hormone testosterone that circulates around our bodies and triggers puberty, in the case of the skin it does not fit perfectly into the hormonal lock. In fact, it has to be modified in the skin—filed for an even better fit. The locksmith that alters the testosterone key is called 5 alpha reductase, and the superactive male hormone that can now turn the lock in record time is known by the abbreviation DHT. It is this key and its maker, 5 alpha reductase, that make men the hairy creatures they are. Hair follicles in the beard and chest region, nose, ears, and in the pubic area are preprogramed to react to DHT by making hairs grow. Men with smooth chests or who have difficulty in growing a beard either have fewer hormone locks in the relevant skin areas or have lazy locksmiths who don't produce enough DHT. Men and women with acne have two to twenty times more DHT in their skin than normal, which makes the skin oily and encourages bacteria to grow.

But what about male pattern baldness? It seems that in these men, thanks to the baldness genes, there are too many locksmiths making too many copies of the DHT keys. The result is that instead of encouraging the growth of new hair, the process is switched off and baldness develops. Why this happens only in the scalp and not in other areas of the body is still not known.

PUBIC HAIR: ITS USES AND ABUSES

Thanks largely to the invention of the zipper, men much more than women have been made conscious of their pubic hair. Members of the male sex are all too painfully aware that hurried visits to the men's room carry the inevitable risk of tearing out great tufts of genital hair. Unfortunately public restrooms are not the most appropriate places for emitting sudden screams of agony, even if those in torment would surely only arouse feelings of silent sympathy from an understanding audience. This negative aspect of having pubic hair has been the butt of many jokes and funny stories for many years. In most cases it is the woman who is ridiculed and often in a discriminatory way.

> A woman confided in her doctor that she needed a cheap operation to make her scream and carry on like a virgin on her wedding night. The doctor's solution was to tie tiny knots in her pubic hair!

Many an intense episode of oral sex has been punctuated by a pregnant pause as the ardent lover attempted to extricate himself from an unwanted pubic hair, and uncontrollable bouts of spitting are not generally considered to enhance an intimate erotic atmosphere. The pubic hair is also the home of those wee little beasties, pubic lice, affectionately known as crabs on account of the horrible little claws they use to hang on to the curly hairs of their host. The dreaded itch, which appears a few days after a casual sexual encounter, can mean only one thing: crabs have landed! The graffiti that often graces the walls of public toilets tells us much of the general attitude towards this pubic parasite . . .

> It ain't no use standing on the seat,
> The crabs in here jump twenty feet

The love of certain men for pubic hair, especially that belonging to the opposite sex, has not gone unnoticed. Many a pubic hair has ended its days as a battle trophy in somebody's secret collection, undeniable evidence of a conquest. The most extreme example of this fetish is described in a book about the famous Wig Club, an exclusive sex club formed in England in the eighteenth century to satisfy the lusty needs of the nobility of the time. The wig, from which the club took its name, was said to have been made from the pubic hair of King Charles II's mistresses, and was added to by all new members. It is said that initiates had to wear this unusual hairpiece, exposing their penis and masturbating publicly on a silver platter to the sound of a ceremonial trumpet.

But pubic hairs don't grow on trees, and many a frustrated fetishist had to find substitutes to turn him on sexually. Hair brushes were a poor alternative, even if you did have a good imagination. In the German states in the late 1800s, when all manner of sexual deviations were commonplace, the velvet and fur fetishists practiced their perversions almost with an air of respectability. After all, it was the upper class who had access to the stuff. Freud believed that for these men, some of whom achieved orgasm just by touching the material, fur and velvet unconsciously symbolized the female pubic hair. The German states must have been the leading importer of velvet underwear and producer of fur-lined toilet paper.

Pubic hair comes in all colors, shapes, and lengths depending on your race and whatever genes you borrowed from your parents. Pubic hairs never lie and any doubts about whether your partner is really a natural blonde can be satisfied by viewing the "mound of Venus."

As you would expect, it is the sex hormones that are responsible for cultivating pubic hair and getting them to sprout at the right time. The male sex hormone, testosterone, is the generator in both sexes, in the boy from the testicles and in the girl from the adrenal gland. Men who, because of a genetic freak of nature, are unable to respond to this hormone do not have pubic hairs; women who have adrenal glands that do not function properly also may have sparse pubic hair. On the other hand, little boys and girls who have too much of the male hormone can develop pubic hair at incredibly young ages, as early as eighteen months. What is interesting is that the distribution of the pubic hair is also very much dependent on how much male hormone is circulating in the body. In men, too little hormone produces an inverted triangle pattern that one associates with women. In women, too much testosterone produces the typical male distribution with a narrow band of hairs tapering up towards the navel. A glance at the pubic hair distribution can tell a hormone doctor a lot about your sex hormones.

The Chinese also thought pubic hair told them a lot about

the owner. Black hairs like feathers of a glossy bird meant a strong and obstinate woman; brown hairs with golden tints meant an easy and generous woman; fine, silky, and short meant quiet and retiring; thick and bushy hairs sweeping down and under the anus spelled passion with sexual juices flowing like a waterfall. If you were really unlucky you could meet a woman with pubic hairs that were patchy and dry, "like vegetation on the top of a hill." Then you'd wish you'd stayed at home. It's unfortunate that Chinese women were not similarly equipped with an easy reference guide to male pubic hair. Back in the Middle Ages in Europe, straight pubic hair was a sign of too much masturbation, which presumably accounts for the popularity of miniature hair curlers at the time.

After spending centuries trying desperately to hide our genital hairs, maybe the time is ripe for a pubic revolution.

Several fashion pioneers have noted how untidy the average pubic area is and advocated pubic combs, sprays, and regular trips to the hairdressers to try to put a little style in our genital grooming. Who knows, the time of pubic wigs and punky pubes may be just around the corner.

SLAVES TO THE MALE HORMONE, TESTOSTERONE

On the surface no two men are alike. Each is a unique combination of physical, emotional, and intellectual traits. What makes them belong to the same club is that curious attribute called maleness, a characteristic that has taken millions of years to evolve and a feature we share with countless others of animal types. Maleness refers not only to muscular arms, hairy chins, and bulges between the legs. It also assumes certain forms of behavior in the sexual and social sphere.

Complex patterns of behavior were programed into primitive brains eons ago, designed to help our ancestors to survive, to reproduce, to compete—urges, drives, and reflexes that are becoming increasingly out of place in our so-called civilized world. Deep within all men is a Rambo imprisoned and shackled by society's rules and regulations. This anachronism, this prototype of maleness, is created by a strange union between the primitive areas of our brains and the male hormone testosterone produced by the testicles. This hormone is the reason for maleness, affecting not only how men look, but to a great extent the fuel to those primitive male pursuits. It may be at a soccer match, with angry hordes of youths tearing each other apart. It may be at a discotheque, with men indulging in courtship displays to entice the defenseless female into their webs. It may be on the road, driving mechanical steeds in life-and-death ego races. It may be at work, involved in power struggles for status and salary. Even within society's prison walls, we are slaves to the irresistible charms and effects of the male hormone, and when the man does his male dance it's his testicles and their released hormone, testosterone, that usually call the tune.

The testicles begin this process of subjugation long before men are born, in fact as early as eight weeks after they have been conceived. Only two weeks after they have been created, the testicles begin to spew out the sex chemical that sows the seeds of the male sex organs and then directs the developing brain according to male patterns. By establishing special combinations of electrical circuits, testosterone programs specific areas of the brain to equip the developing fetus for any future male role in the theater of life.

What happens when little girls are given an overdose of male sex chemical during their mother's pregnancy? This can happen if the mother has taken a special kind of hormone treatment during pregnancy or because the fetus develops a special form of tumor. When these little girls make their debut, the doctor or midwife often has to think twice whether the baby should wear blue or pink, because the baby girl's clitoris can be as large as a baby boy's penis. The interesting thing is that even if these babies are surgically or medically treated, and even if they are raised as little girls, when they get older they often display typical tomboy behavior. They prefer jeans to frilly dresses, prefer to play with bricks rather than little dolls, and prefer to punch little boys on the nose rather than play mommy and daddy.

What happens to little boys when they receive the same overdose? As you might guess, they burst into the world as mini-Rambos who later revel in rough-and-tumble activities and who often become keenly interested in sports. The message seems to be that little boys are usually born with a degree of maleness that falls short of the supermales our chromosomes would have us be. Presumably this helps explain why there exist so many shades of maleness in a normal society, from the guy who gets sand kicked in his face at the beach to the primitive mountain of muscles who does the kicking.

After sowing the seeds of maleness into their host's body during pregnancy and shortly after birth, the testicles take a holiday for around eight years in preparation for the second awakening—puberty. During puberty, those seeds burst into full bloom. It is a time for hairy chins, inferiority complexes, aggression, wet dreams, identity crises, and masturbation. The testicles strike a tune and the male dance has begun. Not only do the testicles have the potential for transforming immature bodies into fighting sex machines . . . with muscles, hair, and those other important extras, but also like wicked demons intent on mischief they whisper dirty thoughts into his ears and implant sexy dreams into his head.

An American study showed that one could predict from the levels of testosterone in the blood of a group of teenagers whether they had begun to have sexy dreams, masturbate, or have sex. In some boys, because of a certain type of cancer, the testicles awake from their hibernation all too early, even at the nursery school age. These mighty midgets grow genitals that can make their fathers green with envy. They often terrorize other children with their aggressive behavior and make life uncomfortable for the teachers with their sexual advances. Imagine telling a five-year-old that the relationship wouldn't work "because of the difference in our ages."

Everybody knows that boys' voices fall in pitch at puberty, an effect of male hormone on their vocal apparatus. Why? one may ask. For many animals, sound is a means of communicating sex. When the boar sings his *chant de coeur* (song of the heart) it makes the females more receptive to his sexual demands. Anybody who has seen a Tarzan film has heard that well-known yell of machismo as Tarzan swings through the trees looking for Jane. Now try to imagine Tarzan doing the same routine with a falsetto voice and you'll get the point. What is not generally appreciated is that the depth of an adult man's voice can say a lot about how much testosterone is circulating around his body. In a German study of male singers between twenty and forty years of age, those with the higher voices (the tenors) had lower levels of testosterone than the baritones, who had in turn less male hormone than those singing bass. Not only that, but the bass singers had sex more often than the other singers and also had bigger feet! Maybe women should invite male suitors to sing a few bars of "Old Man River" before drawing back the bedsheets.

Another aspect of this cocktail of maleness that appears at puberty is aggression, directed toward parents, toward authority, toward themselves, and later even toward other societies. That the testicles are involved in the appearance of aggression and hostility in men has been known for centuries. Certain cannibal tribes ate the testicles of those they slew in battle to acquire their courage, rather like those who ate their victims' brains so that they could be wiser. It is common for critics of a man who lacks the courage or toughness to do something to say, "He didn't have the balls to do it." Primitive farmers learned very quickly how to prevent their stock from becoming aggressive when they went through puberty: They simply cut off their balls. Some have suggested the same technique be used as an alternative means of curbing the rise in societal violence when all else fails.

In a study of ice hockey players in the United States, coaches were asked to rank their players according to how much aggression they showed in their play. Sure enough, those with the worst record for bone-crunching checks and tearing pieces out of the opposition also had the highest testosterone levels in their blood. Studies have also shown that the most violent criminals in prison society, the aggressive psychopaths and violent rapists, often have more sex hormone than other felons.

But what about the man in the street? The guy who stares death rays at you because he doesn't like your tie or the way you breathe, or the guy who threatens you with strangulation simply because you took his parking place—are these Neanderthals also slaves to their testicles? The answer is uncertain.

In at least five different studies based on a questionnaire, researchers have shown that men who are easily irritated or who react violently to provocation have higher levels of sex hormones than the quiet types. But other researchers have not been able to confirm this. This leaves us with the possibility that the testicles may be the culprits in extreme cases of aggression, but that within the normal boundaries of hostile behavior other factors may be more important, for example the combination of small testicles and no brains.

When a man loses his testicles, by accident or design, or if he is treated with a special drug to stop his sex hormone from having any effect, he loses his sexual desire. This principle has been used for many years in the treatment of rapists, child molesters, and sex maniacs. Inject him with testosterone again and his sexual fantasies and his interest in sex make a miraculous comeback.

Anabolic steroids are a form of testosterone taken by athletes to increase their muscle size and strength. However, it is not only on the athletic track that these drugs improve performance. One Swedish athlete must have sent lots of little old ladies into a faint when he announced in the popular press that after a course of steroid treatment he felt so lustful that on one occasion he had sex seventeen times before coming up for air. Understandably, politicians have made it as difficult as possible for the average person to get hold of this precious stuff.

Some men have better success and more sex with women than others. The burning question is, "Do lustful guys have more testosterone than the others?" A group of single American men were followed for one year and records were kept every time they had sex. After the study was over the scientists measured the levels of sex hormone in their blood. The findings were clear. Those lucky in love were not more male, at least judged from their sex hormones, than their more unsuccessful competitors. Once again we are left with the conclusion that within the normal limits of maleness, factors other than the level of testosterone floating around in our blood decide how sexually active we will be. (A gentle smile and a red Porsche may be the secret.) On the other hand, at least one American study has shown that the frequency of masturbation and intercourse in a male population can be closely correlated with seasonal shifts in the circulating testosterone. Is this the ultimate proof of the workings of our hormonal puppet master on our behavior? Or are the alterations in the male hormone the result of variations in our sexual life, not the cause?

What will disappoint many feminists is that scientists now believe that the male hormone may also be responsible for sexual desire in women as well as men. A woman does not need her ovaries to have an interest in sex. But if you surgically remove her adrenal glands, which are the main source of the small amounts of male hormone produced in her body, even an offer from a handsome movie star would be turned down. Women who receive male hormone to destroy a certain type of breast cancer have been reported to have an increased desire for sex. And studies of married couples have shown that those having sex more frequently are those in which the woman has been shown to have higher testosterone levels than average for the female population. The hormone levels in the man did not appear to determine how often they had sex. What's more interesting is that these same women reported a greater level of sexual satisfaction and more easily made friends than other women. Such is the magic of the male sex hormone. So convincing are these types of studies that gynecologists now contemplate treating middle-aged women not only with female sex hormone when they go through menopause, but also with a dash of testosterone to spice up their sex lives and keep their husbands wondering.

Man has come a long way from those days when he could play out his primitive, chauvinistic role as a Tarzan or a Rambo. Now in smart suit and tie he bows to the diplomacy and etiquette of his modern culture. Let us not forget, however, that within this shell of respect and silent obedience are two small organs poised to exploit the times when he or his society relaxes its rules, when once again he can become a slave to the male hormone.

2

THE MALE
SEX MACHINE

6 SEX AND THE MALE BODY

SEX, MAGIC, AND THE SUPERNATURAL

Sex must have appeared magical to the primitive mind, as it does often to the civilized. Puberty was a time when an uncanny effervescence began to bubble in the blood and fermented a transformation not only of the bodily kind but far more strange surgings lower down, unaccountable feelings that blazed through the arteries and fired the flesh. During intercourse, lovers became as if possessed, orgasm a unique state of consciousness in which they became strangely oblivious to surroundings and entered a fleeting trancelike state. The final release caused depletion, loss of vitality as if drained from the very soul. No wonder that for our ancestors sex was hand in hand with the supernatural, not only for procreation but to acquire magical power, a direct channel to life's mysteries and forbidden forces.

For centuries men and women were mystically drawn together for the sexual act without understanding what caused this magnetism, why their bodies reacted in the way they did and what the point of it all was. The old sages in their wisdom attempted to explain the mechanisms of sex,

51

their theories desperately trying to bridge the void between the physical changes they could see and their metaphysical and supernatural significance. Many of their theories were adopted by many of the Eastern philosphies and religions, such as Taoism in China and Tantrism in India. In these parts of the world it was generally held that man and woman possessed in their bodies a vital energy distilled from all bodily organs. The woman had unlimited supplies of this essence of life, but during sex her lover could cheekily steal some of this energy through her saliva in a kiss and through her sex organ secretions during intercourse. There was one little problem: If our passionate lover ejaculated, this precious energy would be lost forever in his seed. With each orgasm his body became more and more drained of its vitality. The unfortunate man was destined for an early death and sickness. The only way to avoid the inevitable was to have sex without orgasm, and techniques were developed so that he could do just that—a strong will was clearly not enough.

There was an added bonus. Each time he managed to bite his lip and send his ejaculate back to where it came from he came one step closer to immortality. Intercourse was like a strong breeze fanning a glowing ember that could suddenly burst into a flame of vitality that spread up his spinal cord to fire his brain, to stimulate his intellect, prolong his life, and even give him insight into a world beyond. A mere one thousand episodes of intercourse without orgasm and our man could live forever, which illustrates the difficulty of the task. The Indian mystics described this infusion of energy in a wonderfully symbolic way. In an area of the male body that we now believe was roughly where the prostate sits was a sleeping snake coiled eight times. During sex, as the vital energy was passed from the woman into the man, this snake, or Kundalini as it was called, was a form of sexual energy that began to stir and ascend the spinal cord on its way to the brain. A lapse in concentration, and even the teeniest ejaculation sent it slithering back to its sleepy abode. Anal sex sent the Kundalini in the opposite direction, which indicates how much this form of sex was frowned upon in the East.

THE EARLY SEX RESEARCHERS

What was happening in the West while the wise men of the East were wrestling with their theories on sex? Aristotle, a keen observer, could not ignore the movements of the male buttocks during intercourse. It was clear to him that they must be of vital importance, acting like bellows to propel the male seed out of the body. Aside from him and a few others, the majority with crackpot ideas, our understanding of the sexual act moved at a snail's pace. The church did not help matters. Any aspiring sex researcher had to look twice over his shoulder before taking notes or he risked incurring the wrath of a bishop or two.

One person who took the helm against these tidal waves of ignorance and bigotry in the West was Albertus Magnus, a thirteenth-century sex revolutionary. He took notes and he dared to tell of his findings. He saw that the clitoris was no more than a miniature penis, to which he gave a common name, virga. What he could see of the female sex organs on the outside reminded him of an uplifted scrotum and he wrote of their similarity to the male organs. He marveled at the way the testicles moved closer into the body during intercourse and reasoned that this would make it easier to expel the male seed. He wrote that slight sexual stimulation produced a substance in both sexes that he believed was halfway between seed and sweat, produced in a man by the touch of a woman with whom he would like to have intercourse. His observations and ideas heralded a new era in man's understanding of the sex act, but men like Magnus were few and far between. In the centuries that followed his work, the dark secrets of sex remained hidden, revealed only to inquisitive lovers conducting their own experiments.

Like a breath of fresh air came the seventeenth century with a new generation of scientists, men given not to wild theories based on scanty observation but who relied on experiment and objective recording of data. These were men like the anatomist Regnier de Graaf. With each stroke of his dissecting knife, de Graaf cut away the magic and superstition that clouded man's understanding of the sex act. Blood was the basis of erection. He knew this because when he tied a piece of thread around the base of the erect penis of a dog that had recently mated, and then cut it off, he saw that it was filled with blood. He showed this even more convincingly when, by filling the amputated penises of his corpses with water, he could make them erect just as in life. He dissected men killed during the act of intercourse, presumably by a jealous husband, and saw the amazing way the sex glands had swollen almost to bursting as if in preparation for an ejaculation that would never come. He made sensible observations such as "the penis is located at the bottom of the belly so sex may take place more comfortably."

But while other men like de Graaf were making great strides in other disciplines, the sad truth is that when he dried the blood from his scalpel for the last time, sex research ground to a halt. In fact we had to wait three hundred years before this taboo was lifted sufficiently for scientists to take an objective peek at an activity they themselves had been enjoying for many years. As one would expect, the first observations didn't exactly rock the scientific world and certainly would not have impressed the man in the street if he had been told. One of the first bodily changes observed to occur during intercourse, aside from the obvious ones associated with the sex organs, was that heart rate increased. The first attempts to measure heart rate scientifically during sex date back to 1896 when Dr. Kolb was wondering what other things to measure with his ECG machine. It took fifty years before Klumbies and Kleinsorge added that sex increased blood pressure and also caused heavy breathing. It was only when the sex gurus Masters and Johnson turned an academic eye to lovemaking that sex was finally brought from the shadows into the glaring spotlight of the laboratory.

MASTERS AND JOHNSON TAKE SEX RESEARCH INTO THE MODERN AGE

Over a period of twelve years, Masters and Johnson observed and recorded more than 10,000 male and female orgasms. In their first studies they used prostitutes as subjects. Later, they collected data from nonprofessional volunteers, almost 700 of them. Their original findings form the basis of what we know today about the bodily reactions to intercourse.

AN AFFAIR OF THE HEART

As indicated above and as any romantic would arrest, sex is basically a matter of the heart, or more correctly the cardiovascular system. Miniature valves opened by cerebral command send an increased volume of blood coursing through the veins, erecting and swelling nipples and sex organs by a touch, by the sight or even by the thought of a lover. The heart has always been associated with love and sex, probably because its pulse rate changes with arousal and passion. Most of Masters and Johnson's information was obtained by filming couples having intercourse and by using relatively simple means for recording the accompanying bodily changes. Since these classical studies, scientists have to an increasing extent made use of modern technology to help them in their thirst for sexual knowledge. Small electronic sensors were placed strategically in and around sex organs, surreptitiously sending sex's hidden secrets to researchers in white lab coats in an adjacent room. Under these conditions, sex was surely less artificial.

The most obvious circulatory change observed by Masters and Johnson was vasocongestion, the pooling of blood in certain organs. Aside from the penis and clitoris, the most obviously affected organ was the breasts—of both sexes. Nipple erection occurs as a result of the contraction of small muscles that can make the nipples protrude an extra ¼ to ⅜ inch, but the increase in breast volume (on average 20 percent) is due to the increase in its blood content. Armed with a ruler and a steady hand the sexologists also discovered that, like the penis, big nipples erected less than their normal-sized cousins. Another example of localized blood pooling they observed during sex is the measles-like reaction, the sex flush, that spreads over the chest and breasts during the preorgasmic period, and then magically disappears almost immediately after orgasm. This red reaction, caused by the dilation of small blood vessels in the skin, occurs in 75 percent of women and 25 percent of men at climax. The more intense the sexual response of the woman, the greater the blushing and the redder she becomes. In certain cases, this blushing reaction can spread down her back and down to her thighs. In men, the flush comes a little later, not so frequently (25 percent of the cases), and when it does is more confined to the neck and face. They are undeniable signs that a partner has been enjoying the session and not simply faking it. Today these blood changes can be observed indirectly using sophisticated techniques like thermography or thermistors, which measure the amount of heat given off by various body parts, which in turn reflects their blood flow. By using special whole-body cameras, sex researchers have mapped the temperature and blood flow of naked subjects during masturbation or after seeing erotic films. The studies indicate that when somebody gets turned on, his or her belly gets cold, the skin over the chest gets warm, and, as expected, the sex organ gets hot, one to two degrees higher than the body temperature. This cooling of the skin over the belly, which reflects divergence of blood to the sex organs, has also been measured using small electronic sensors, thermistors, clipped to the skin, and has been recommended as a convenient method of recording sexual excitement. Similar drops in temperature also occur in the fingers when subjects watch pornographic films apparently for the same reasons: diversion of blood to more important parts!

MORTE DOUCE—THE SWEET DEATH

It is clear that with all these adjustments in the distribution of blood in the body, not only to the sex organs but also to skin and to pumping muscles, the heart must work faster and the pulse rate must inevitably rise: from a rate of 70 at rest to an impressive 180 beats a minute at orgasm followed by a steep fall. This fact has encouraged some sex researchers to use coital heart rate as an indication that orgasm has occurred. This increasing rhythm during the sexual act may explain why such music as "The Theme of Fate" in *Carmen* is considered to be so erotic, with its heartlike drumbeats gradually building up to an orgasmic crescendo. The long list of men, including Attila the Hun, who have died of heart attacks while performing sex has surely reminded many that sex is not a spectator sport. In fact, according to Mohammed, to die in the glorious battle abed with one's belly on top is to die a martyr of love. Christian wisemen have viewed things differently, seeing death during the sexual act as the ultimate wickedness.

For many cardiologists, the potential extra load on the heart occurring during sex is worrisome: 20 percent of post-cardiac patients have angina during sex. On the other hand, several more sympathetic studies have shown that for a middle-aged man alone with his wife, the modest increase in heart rate during sex should cause no problem—no more than going up a flight of stairs. The problem arises when the same middle-aged man swaps his wife for another woman. In Japan, 0.6 percent of all sudden deaths could be blamed on heart attacks during sex. In almost all cases, the deceased were discovered in motel rooms, invariably in bed with a prostitute, the only witness. It seems that the extra excitement of an illicit love affair can prove too much for some middle-aged hearts. It has been rightly pointed out by others that owing to the delicacy of the situation it may more often be covered up when it occurs at home. Unfortunately, our would-be unfaithful husband can not avoid a coronary simply by being a more passive sex partner, because a study in 1976 showed that the position adopted during sex has little to say for the strain on the heart: the heart of a man on the bottom beats just as fast as when he is on top. Happily, sudden death or heart attack during intercourse are rarely reported in women. The significance of these findings can only be guessed!

HEAVY BREATHING AND THE SEXUAL ARIA

Working muscles need oxygen, hence the heavy breathing during sex. The first sexologists observed breathing rates of up to forty per minute at orgasm in pairs having sexual intercourse. What intrigued some scientists more than the breathing was the moans associated with it. In female monkeys and to a lesser extent in human females, the heavy, rhythmical breathing associated with sex is usually associated with bursts of sound that synchronize with the breathing. Using sophisticated recording equipment a characteristic print of this erotic aria has been made. Orgasm in the females of both species can be associated with an intense cacophony of calls that in the case of our ape cousins can be heard over long distances. In contrast, men and male monkeys were remarkable for their reticence to join with their mates in a love duet. There were grunts, yes, but usually only at orgasm.

Why do monkeys especially and humans to a lesser extent vocalize during sex? Two intriguing explanations have been offered. During intercourse men find it increasingly difficult to hold back their ejaculation when they hear the crescendo of orgasmic moans coming from their partners. The idea is that both come at the same time to increase the chances that their partners will become pregnant since at orgasm the shape of the vagina is optimal for keeping the semen in contact with the cervix. What better way of ensuring this than by imprinting in the male brain the erotic significance of her sexual moans? The second explanation for the woman's sex aria is that it is left over from the time when we were swinging in the trees and when sex was not monogamous but invariably a gang bang with five to ten males being involved. The authors argue that the orgasmic moans coming from the female could be heard by other eager suitors in the neighborhood, who then formed a line.

GETTING ALL TENSE

Masters and Johnson noted two other bodily changes associated with sex that did not involve the genitals. One of these was myotonia, an increase in tension of the body's muscles. Such a buildup in tension could be seen in the form of regular contractions or spasms of certain muscle groups. The sex gurus noted the way the subjects of both sexes frowned, scowled, and grimaced as their facial muscles contracted in an uncontrollable manner reflecting this buildup of sexual tension and a reaching for release. They noticed that the neck muscles also contracted in a spasmodic and uncontrollable way, first keeping the neck rigidly in midposition during the first phases of intercourse and then throwing the head backward as climax was reached. This backward movement was especially noted in the person on top.

In fact, hardly any of the body's muscles lay idle during these sex sessions. They saw how women drew their knees together as orgasm approached, a movement that can be particularly uncomfortable for men performing oral sex. At the point of orgasm, they observed loss of control, with the body acting like some runaway machine, as if something deep in the primitive recesses of our brains had taken over. It was as though the muscles followed preprogramed movements designed to deposit semen deep in the vagina. The man begins to thrust vigorously and deeply, tightening the muscles in his thighs and buttocks. At that time, Masters and Johnson obtained their data on muscle tension by analyzing movies of copulating pairs. Today scientists use small needle electrodes that they stick under the skin to record this buildup in tension. One published study using muscular tension as a measure of orgasmic response took a look at the effects of alcohol on the performance of a group of masturbators. Their studies showed (and I'm sure many men could confirm) that a double whisky not only made it harder for the men to reach an ejaculation (almost three times longer than usual) but also made their orgasms less intense. These men generally felt less stimulated by erotic films. It's certainly true that many a woman has been pleasantly surprised by the staying power of her male partner after a moderate drinking session—assuming she can wake him up, that is!

POST COITUS OMNE ANIMAL TRISTE EST

One fascinating way nature increases the chances of conception is the phase of relaxation that invariably follows a sexual encounter, the time when lovers lie back and languidly blow smoke rings seen through glazed eyes. The Romans had an appropriate way of describing it—*Post coitus omne animal triste est* ("After intercourse all creatures are sad). In the same way that a heavy meal is often followed by forty winks so that the digestive process can continue undisturbed by unnecessary bodily activity, the sudden release of sexual tension during orgasm can send lovers into a deep slumber almost instantaneously. In fact, certain cynics have suggested that sex is a convenient way of curing insomnia. It is during this time that sperm cells can make good an unhindered escape from their pool into the dark recesses of the female body. Any movement at this time, especially initiated by a hard-to-satisfy male partner, could interfere with the formation of the seminal pool and reduce the chances of pregnancy.

ANAL VIBRATIONS

As mentioned earlier, learned men have been interested in the role of the anus in the sexual act for many hundreds of years, more specifically in the role of the muscles around the anus. These muscles belong to the same system that serves the sex organs and share the nerves that coordinate both the male and female orgasms. Sex physiologists have studied the anus in several ways. Masters and Johnson simply unashamedly watched very closely and saw that when their subjects had an orgasm the muscles around the anus contracted two to five times—approximately once a second—and that the more intense the orgasm, the more obvious the anal response. Having a stranger peer into your nether parts during sex can't have helped the subjects' concentration, so scientists developed other more subtle ways of getting their information—such as needle electrodes delicately placed in the muscles surrounding the anus, or anal probes, air balloons placed in the anus that when squeezed by the pulsating anus send out electric signals that reflect the intensity of the contractions. Using this device, astounding results were obtained. It was found that the male anus contracts not two to five times but a magnificent fifteen to twenty times during an average orgasm of 25.8 seconds.

Using anal probes and a technique for measuring heart rate, other scientists discovered a new phenomenon in male sexual biology—the multiple orgasm. Most men are aware that orgasm and ejaculation occur at the same time, most often followed by a period during which the penis falls into a deep deep sleep, to be awakened only by the kiss of a beautiful princess (after at least thirty minutes), or so the fairy tale goes. In actual fact this need not be the case. Studies have discovered an incredibly happy group of men who are capable of having three to ten complete orgasms before ejaculation—in one case thirty orgasms in one hour. Somehow these lucky fellows can inhibit the wave of muscular movement that shoots the ejaculate out of the body.

"BETTER THAN TWO ASPIRINS"

Animal experiments have shown that during stimulation of the sexual organs, the pain threshold in the male and female increases to the point that one would believe the animals had been injected with a large dose of morphine. Laughing gas is known to increase the levels of morphinelike pain-killers, the endorphins, in our brains; a South African study showed that one whiff of this gas during intercourse not only made the women laugh but also intensified their orgasms. Treatment with a drug called naloxone, which is known to hinder the action of these pain-killers, prevented the orgasm from happening. What is more is that the site in the brain that triggers orgasm also happens to be the area containing the highest levels of these natural morphines. The obvious conclusion from these findings is that these chemicals are in some way responsible for the feelings associated with our sexual climaxes. If so, it certainly weakens the old excuse "Not tonight, honey, I have a headache" because modern research would suggest that sex cures a headache just as well as a couple of aspirins.

HORMONES AND SEX

Sex causes profound changes in blood hormone levels. In men, intercourse is associated with an increase in the male sex hormone testosterone in the blood. In fact just looking at an erotic movie can increase the amount of testosterone in our body fluids such as saliva. Interestingly, in one study, a film of somebody getting his teeth drilled sent the same hormone plummeting in the opposite direction. During orgasm in both sexes, nerve chemicals suddenly spill into the bloodstream in large amounts, a testimony to the intensity of nervous excitement. Strange substances with strange names like VIP believed to be involved in redirecting blood in different organs also leak into the blood. Oxytocin, another hormone that is released during sex, appears to be responsible for the uterine contractions during orgasm and may also be involved in orgasm in men. The list of hormones and chemicals shown to be involved in human sexual response grows longer every year, an indication of the shock waves that sex sends cursing through our bodies.

In an orgasm-obsessed culture like the one we are supposed to have today, those who have sexual problems soon make themselves heard, a challenge eagerly met by researchers and clinicians . . . and talk-show hosts. A prerequisite for obtaining help is a greater understanding of the bodily changes that occur during problem-free sex. Some science-fiction writers have predicted a cold and sterile future when every family will have a pleasure booth, standing between the microwave oven and dishwasher, in which sex sensations can be experienced at the push of a button. Body energy is channeled into cerebral activities instead of such primitive acts as intercourse. A future free from performance anxiety, sexual conflicts, jealousy, impotence, frigidity—a wonderful vision?

7 ERECTIONS: THE PENIS AS MAN'S DISOBEDIENT SERVANT

Most men have experienced the uncanny way their sex organs appear to have a will of their own. Embarrassing moments, best forgotten when, at the heights of sexual frenzy, and moans of invitation are at their most intense, our sexual organ remains hidden from sight, like some spoiled child who suddenly decides it doesn't want to come out to play after all. And there are the other occasions when we wake up in the morning to find our moody appendage standing erect and stony hard, and no member of the opposite sex is within sight. This is even more surprising when the owner's only recollection of dreams that night was a replay from yesterday's football game. In adolescence, a single kiss is enough to keep a penis hard for a whole day, while as the years roll by, that organ apparently becomes more fickle, a lot more discerning, and sometimes downright resistant to any amount of erotic bribery.

As Plato wrote, "In man the nature of the genital organs is disobedient and self-willed, like a creature deaf to reason and it attempts to dominate all because of its frenzied lusts." In recognition of the existence of this other entity, men began to give their sexual organs their very own identities, calling them names such as Manfred or (in England)

John-Thomas or Willy or Percy. The use of such nicknames enabled lovers to shift the blame for any poor performance in bed on "Manfred, who hasn't been feeling too well lately."

Nature, in its wisdom, gave man a dual-purpose organ combining the function of urination with that of transferring semen deep into the woman's vagina during intercourse. This attempt at saving space obviously created problems—the penis had to be stiff and long for sex, but relaxed for emptying the bladder. A permanently stiff penis suffers from certain drawbacks, not least being that toilets would have to be redesigned and the carrying of umbrellas mandatory at all public restrooms. Regnier de Graaf, in the seventeenth century, put it better: "It would be unseemly and disgusting, and it would totally impede one's conduct in wordly affairs to be like the Satyrs and have a penis always erect. On the other hand, to have one always loose and floppy would incommode successful conduct of the affairs of Venus." What then causes this transformation from the weak and humble Dr. Jekyll to the monstrous and rampant Mr. Hyde?

THE ERECTION CIRCUIT

As any sailor knows, getting a hard-on is not under the control of the will—like moving an arm or leg—although I have heard stories about Indian swamis who can do amazing things with their penises just by concentrating on their navel. The truth is that the penis performs on reflex, which is why it can surprise us by popping up from nowhere when least expected.

An interesting illustration of the lack of conscious control we have over the erection process is provided by night erections or "nocturnal penile tumescence." On average, men get erections during their sleep approximately every 70 to 100 minutes, the intervals growing longer as we get older. They are the result of a general explosion of activity in certain nerves that are beyond our control. Measurements of these erections during sleep help physicians differentiate among the different types of impotence.

Erection is the result of the activity of a set of nerves that emerge from the base of the spinal cord—let us for simplicity call them the "erection" nerves. There is also another set of nerves—let's call them the "softy" nerves—plugged into the penis, and it is these that have been many a man's downfall. Of course there are also other nerves, such as the sensitive ones on the head of the penis sending messages that something nice is going on down there.

The indication that erection has a lot to do with reflexes that are not under our control comes unhappily from accident victims who have been paralyzed after breaking their backs. Despite extensive paralysis, a surprisingly large number of these men, 80 to 90 percent, are capable of erection, often in the absence of electrical contact between the brain and the sex organs. The closer the damage of the spinal cord to the head, the better the chances of becoming erect. Whereas normally, a sexy dream, a flash of thigh, sensual sounds, or a whiff of the right perfume can rouse the penis to life (indicating that the brain is plugged into the erection circuit), with these spine-injured men, erection is brought about by making use of more primitive reflexes below the belt. This can be achieved, for example, by stimulating the head of the penis using a vibrator or touching certain trigger points on the inner side of the thighs or under the testicles. In this case, the electrical signals take a shortcut, from the sensitive nerves in the penis to the spine and from there back out again to the penis to the "erection" nerves controlling the erection. The problem is that, because the brain is not tuned in, one minute the penis may be up and the next it may be down.

Interestingly, in healthy men there can from time to time occur short circuits in the system from parallel circuits in adjacent organs such as the bladder. Signals from a full bladder can hop over to the "erection" nerves and give many men a confusing erection. Magnus Hirschfield, the nineteenth-century sexologist, described a married homo-sexual whose ability to perform the sexual act with his wife and make her pregnant was entirely dependent on his morning erections, which are usually thanks to a full bladder. Sudden breaking of the neck is also often associated with a spontaneous erection, a gory observation made by executioners when they hang men sentenced to death. The explanation is still uncertain but may be due to the sudden unplugging of the "softy" nerves. Erection seems to be therefore controlled by reflexes and associations in both places, between the ears and below the belt.

HOW ERECTION OCCURS

Let's recapitulate: our hero is with the woman of his dreams. After an evening of wine and romantic music to dampen his inhibitions, they are alone. The sight of her inviting lips and heaving breasts, the smell of musky perfumes, the sounds of her heavy moans, the touch of her body all create explosions of electrical activity from his senses to a primitive part of the brain called the limbic system. This is the animal in all of us, one of the first parts of the brain to evolve—that part controlling the bodily reflexes associated with fear, hunger, thirst, anger, and, of course, sex. But as these sensations are traveling to the limbic center, other parts of the brain are first "consulted." These other parts are the "memory banks," the association centers (Are these body signals he is registering from her really an invitation to sex?), centers of conscience, morality, and guilt (Is it wrong what he is doing now? What would his wife think?), centers associated with his self-image (Is he going to perform well? What does she expect from him?). If the primitive center then gets the green light, the monster takes over and impulses fire like express trains down the spinal cord following a pattern programed into his brain millions of years ago. The "erection" nerves cause the penis to become erect. A touch of the woman's hand to the genital area triggers reflexes that strengthen the erection even more—at least for the time being. As we will see later, those infernal "softy" nerves are never far away.

A MATTER OF HYDRAULICS

How do these "erection" nerves get the penis to stand at attention? Eastern philosophies saw a connection between breathing and sex. Some took this belief one stage further and argued that the process of erection must be based on air, like pumping gas into a balloon. Impotence could be easily explained by a puncture. Indeed, in certain societies there was a ban on gas-producing foods like peas and beans because they were thought to have a pneumatic effect on the sex organ.

In the Middle Ages, Albertus Magnus wrote that erection was caused by a substance he called "Venositas," a gas or a liquid (he wasn't sure which), that "transmitted heat into the genital region causing the male organ to swell and harden." Certain Greeks, who presumably had a special interest in mechanics, had previously come up with the bright idea that the testicles acted like counterweights to raise the penis to the correct angle for penetration.

Today we know that man has a hydraulic penis. Inside the shaft of the penis are three cylinders of sponge, two large cylinders on either side surrounded by a tight coat of fiber that limits their expansion. The third surrounds the urethra and then balloons out at the end to form the head of the penis—the glans. It's important to understand that the blood supplies to the shaft and the head of the penis are quite different and explains why the head of the penis is usually a little softer than the shaft even at the height of sexual excitement. The spaces inside these spongy cylinders are surrounded by a thin layer of muscle that, when contracted, squashes the spaces flat. Because of the resistance offered by these squashed spaces, blood entering the penis takes a U-turn back out again, and the small arteries connecting the sponge spaces are so "dry" that they are coiled like small corkscrews. The nerves that keep the penis deflated in this matter are the "softy" nerves, which are also stress nerves. These are the same nerves responsible for producing adrenaline, and part of the system that is turned on when you are frightened or angry. If you stuck an electrode into a soft penis, it would buzz with activity because these nerves are constantly firing to stop the spongy cylinders from being filled with blood.

One of the ways the "erection" nerves cause the erection is to interfere with the action of the "softy" nerves by producing a chemical that neutralizes their effect. A similar chemical can be injected directly into the penis and do the same thing, creating an erection indistinguishable from the real article. The problem is that the "softy" nerves are much more clever at pulling down the periscope than the other nerves are at getting it up. In fact if both sets are switched on at the same time, the erection nerves never stand a chance and the penis will remain limp. This is the reason why feelings or emotions that strengthen the impulses along these "stress" nerves such as anxiety (Will I perform well?), guilt, and fear (Will her husband come home soon?) are so efficient at screwing up the big night. Not only that, but it's why preoccupation with the job situation, problems with private economy, and the results of the football game all can put the penis off balance. The same stress nerves are also responsible for that strange phenomenon, "the disappearing penis" after a swim in an ice-cold sea.

When the "erection" nerves finally do get their say and neutralize the effects of their opposites, the muscle layer in the sponge tissue relaxes, the blood spaces expand like balloons, and the corkscrew arteries lengthen as they are filled. As the blood spaces expand they squeeze shut the veins carrying blood out of the penis to a trickle, making the erection even firmer. That's why you cannot squeeze the blood from a penis once it is erect. When these veins begin to spring a leak, because they are not flattened enough against the fibrous walls of the penis, the dark clouds of impotence begin to gather. Finally, a set of muscles at the base of the penis contracts to make the blood barrels stretch to the bursting point, making the penis not only bigger but also rigid enough to break through the resistance offered by the driest vagina.

AN EXPANDING INDUSTRY

Vacuum pumps for enlarging the erection are an "expanding" industry in many countries today. The principle of the technique is that, by creating a vacuum around the penis, you can suck additional blood into the sponge tissues and expand it to its maximum size. Some manufacturers' claims—that you can add four inches to the size of the erect organ—should be treated with extreme caution. It should be mentioned that simply using the organ regularly in normal intercourse will theoretically have the same effect. De Graaf in the seventeenth century wrote, "Those who go down with any frequency to fight the battles of Venus are always noticing how frequent copulation greatly increases the size of the penis." Closer to our own time, Hirschfield wrote, "Prolonged indifference to the primal sexual urge will gradually weaken, from lack of use, the sexual mechanism and eventually leads to incompetency. The penis is a muscular organ which needs to be exercised, as do all muscular structures, to be competent." The message is the more you use it, the bigger it gets. The increased production of testosterone that is known to occur after each episode of intercourse may mean that sex not only exercises the penis physically but also gives its tissues a hormone boost that also helps the process.

ERECTION DISTRACTION

Even when an erection is artificially produced by injecting drugs into the penis, it will be stronger when the patient is under complete narcosis or when he injects the drug himself at home. The reason is that the background activity of the stress or "softy" nerves is raised by the general activities around us and serve to reduce the strength of the erection. The child waking up in the night and disturbing his parents in the throes of sex is enough to inhibit the father all night—maybe even the next night if it has happened several times. In some of the studies by Masters and Johnson, the ringing of a bell or the appearance of a new face during the sexual act was enough to send an erection plummeting, the moral being never to have sex in a public place or by the side of a fire station. On the other hand, prolonged foreplay, a quiet room, the gentle sounds of Ravel's *Bolero*, a musky perfume, and a gently chewed ear all remove the effects of the stress nerves and allow the "erection" nerves to do their job of creating an erection as hard as the rock of Gibraltar and twice as thick.

THE AROUSAL INDICATOR

Because he gets an erection, a man's sexual response is much easier to observe and record than that of the female. In today's laboratory it is a relatively simple matter to wrap a strain gauge around the penis and measure the degree to which the rubber band stretches in different situations. Thanks to these sensors, interesting data has been published over the last few years on what turns on the average man and the pervert. Studies using this technique have been used to test the response of child molesters to pictures of naked children and of rapists to scenes of sexual violence.

An interesting application for this erection recorder was to find out whether exposure to too much pornography had an effect on the erection. Volunteers saw ninety minutes of pornography every day for three weeks and once a week were tested using the strain gauge. The result: the erection that the men normally got in response to the porn gradually shriveled as the study continued. But after the men had

had an eight-week holiday and were tested again, their erections were as strong as at the beginning of the study. Others showed that four ten-minute sessions of porn spread over a week had no negative effects on erection. The conclusions were clear: too much porn may not be good for man's sex life.

Modern measuring devices have also shown that alcohol reduces the time it takes to become erect and prolongs the time to orgasm. They have revealed that the size of erections that men get during sleep can be directly related to how much of the male hormone is circulating in the blood. Slowly but surely and thanks to a simple device of rubber and wire, the secrets that men have kept to themselves for thousands of years, their weaknesses, their sexual fears are being laid bare for all to scrutinize.

8 COMING AND GOING: THE MALE SEXUAL CLIMAX

The male climax, unlike that of the female, is in most cases an inevitable part of the sexual act. How long it takes to achieve a climax can reinforce a man's masculine image to granite hardness or tear it into tiny shreds. Modern society has created intolerable demands on our male hero, who has to not only brandish the proper equipment and use it in the right way, but also muster up awesome powers to suppress all those primitive reflexes telling him that Vesuvius is about to erupt. The trick is to achieve mind over matter until a nod and a wink from his now satisfied partner means he can send his payload finally into orbit. How is ejaculation brought about and how does it influence the male orgasm?

ASSEMBLING THE EJACULATE

The release of semen involves two separate acts: emission, equivalent to loading the gun; and ejaculation, firing it. The barrel of the gun in this case is the urethra. At the base of the urethra is the bladder, which has two muscular valves guarding its entrance—an inner valve and an outer valve, with a space in between. This space in between is the chamber of the gun. Emission occurs when the cartridge of secretions from the different sex organs is loaded into this pressure chamber. As will be discussed in a later chapter, the different sex glands don't squeeze their contents into the urethra at exactly the same time. First comes the product of the prostate, then the testicular contribution, and lastly the fluid from the seminal vesicles.

MALE GENITAL SYSTEM

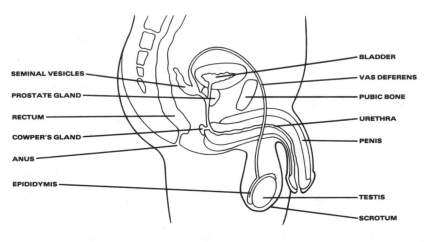

Illustration reprinted with permission from Diagram Visual Information Ltd.

These contributions are somewhat like three small cartridges loaded in sequence. We don't appear to need our brains to do the loading. In fact it's basically a local reflex, triggered by sensory nerves around the penis that are connected to a point in the spinal cord located about halfway between the base of the spine and the base of the ribs. A vibrator placed just under the glans can trigger the reflex and is commonly used as a means of obtaining semen from paraplegic men, who can then impregnate their wives by artificial insemination. In fact emission also occurs in men with amputated penises and here this sensory reflex is impossible. In certain spine-damaged men where there is a one-way traffic of nerve signals down the spinal cord, emission can also be triggered by looking at erotic movies. In the Kinsey report, three or four men were found who could ejaculate simply by concentrating on sexual fantasies without any genital manipulation.

Thanks to the nerves that cause the sex glands to contract, the secretions pour into this closed pressure chamber. During this process, nerves that control the opening and closing of the inner and outer valves of the chamber now close both tightly shut. For a brief moment, the walls of this pressure chamber relax to accommodate the semen. As the walls stretch, sensory nerves send feelings of inevitability to our brain and a point of no return is reached. Ejaculation is imminent.

EJACULATION

The process of ejaculation, during which semen is ejected out of the penis, is, like emission, a complicated reflex depending on a highly coordinated and precisely timed stream of nerve impulses fired from a spinal center. Activation of this center takes place when the pressure chamber is loaded with semen. Muscles at the base of the penis squeeze the pressure chamber by contracting three to seven times at 0.8-second intervals. At the same time the muscular outer door of the pressure chamber relaxes for a brief moment, and the muscles of the pelvic floor contract spasmodically causing the semen to squirt out under high pressure. In diseases of these muscles, although inevitability is felt because emission is in order, the semen just seeps out and the orgasm is less intense. One scientist has noted that the "seminal stream usually covers a distance of from six to eight inches, but it has been known to exceed one yard." In this respect, it's the seventeen- to nineteen-year-olds who'd run off with the gold medal. As age creeps on, the semen volume gets less, the force with which it is ejaculated becomes reduced, and the orgasm becomes a faint shadow of what it once was.

PREMATURE EJACULATION

When animals indulge in the delights of mating they are vulnerable to attack by any meat eater that happens to be passing. To get around the problem, in most species, nature has programed the male so that within a short time of entering the vagina, sensitive receptors on the end of the penis reflexively cause it to ejaculate. After uncoupling, both sexes can then if necessary take evasive action if the carnivore appears. There are of course exceptions. Most of us have seen what happens to dogs when they get locked together during mating, although a bucket of cold water usually works wonders! The boar also appears to be indifferent when he mounts the sow, often going to sleep on the sow's back after he's ejaculated—hardly prepared for evasive action. But in general, thanks to spinal reflexes out of their control, ejaculation in apes such as the gorilla and chimpanzee usually takes place within seconds of penetration.

What about men? Men, on average, ejaculate within two minutes after the start of intercourse, varying between ten seconds to three minutes. This is equivalent to thirty to sixty thrusts. Whether you belong to the sprint or marathon class varies according to age and the situation. The older the person is, the longer he can delay his ejaculation, which can be partly explained by the reduced sensitivity of the head of his penis. On the other hand, regardless of age, a novel situation such as a new partner or long periods of sexual abstinence can turn anybody into an Olympic sprint champion.

One of the desirable attributes of a good lover is the ability to control ejaculation, at least until his partner is satisfied. This involves suppressing the primitive reflex from the penis, presumably by raising the threshold of the ejacula-

tion center in the spine. In our modern, sexually emanci-
pated society, men are under increasing pressure to
overcome this reflex, which has taken nature millions of
years to evolve. It seems that some are better at wrestling
with their spinal reflexes than others.

The clinical criteria for this condition, which is also called
ejaculatio præcox, is that "Ejaculation occurs before the individual wishes it, because of recurrent and persistent absence of reasonable voluntary control of ejaculation and
orgasm during sexual activity." Here the words recurrent
and persistent are important and of course exclude that vast
number of men who experience premature ejaculation only
on the first night. Before stigmatizing the patient with the
"premature ejaculator" label, the doctor must take into account the novelty of the partner, the normal frequency and
duration of sexual intercourse, and the man's age. An eigh-
teen-year-old premature ejaculator who has a different partner every night and uses one hour for foreplay is not
necessarily abnormal. Usually, an authentic premature ejaculator has never learned voluntary control over his ejaculation reflexes and has always "fired" with the least
provocation. He may have such a poor picture of himself
as a lover that he may actually avoid sex. His partner may
feel rejected and desperately unhappy because she wrongly
misinterprets the rapid ejaculation as a sign of her lover's
indifference, while he feels guilty and pressured. Some psychoanalysts have gone so far as to postulate that premature
ejaculation reflects a deep-seated male hostility to women,
an unconscious desire to deprive their partner of pleasure.
A smaller number of men have problems only in special
situations, maybe every time they are with a particular partner. This once again emphasizes how, under normal conditions, the majority of men are putting the brake on their
orgasms. It's interesting that the commonly held superstition that the spilling of salt would bring bad luck also has
a sexual interpretation. According to some psychoanalysts,
salt symbolizes man's semen and the spilling of it, premature ejaculation, may represent an unconscious fear of being labeled a poor lover.

TREATMENT OF PREMATURE EJACULATION

Most men have their own tricks for preventing an ill-timed ejaculation. The usual technique is to concentrate on something else during the sexual act, for example taking nine from a hundred and counting backward, thinking about their taxes or something equally unpleasant such as their in-laws or their boss at work. Others try to reduce the sensitivity of their penis by using an extra-thick condom or spraying the lower half of their bodies with an anesthetic. The late Aly Khan, who suffered seriously from premature ejaculation, had his own novel solution to his problem. By his bed he would keep a champagne ice bucket into which he'd plunge his hand at the moment of crisis. As we will read later, the Chinese developed several methods for delaying or preventing ejaculation. One was to nip the nipple of the right breast (his own not his partner's) and gnash the teeth. Another was to use three fingers to squeeze a point between the scrotum and anus for three to four seconds. The latter was often preferable because he didn't have to withdraw his penis to do it.

Today there are two techniques accepted by the majority of sex therapists: (1.) The "squeeze" technique pioneered by Masters and Johnson and (2.) The "stop-start" technique first described by Semans in the 1950s. In both cases, the partner plays an important role in the therapy. In the "squeeze" technique, the man withdraws his penis when he feels he is about to ejaculate. The partner quickly holds the penis with one thumb on the underside of the glans and two fingers around the circumference and squeezes gently. This stimulates nerves that interfere with the transmission of impulses to the ejaculation center in the spinal cord. It also reduces the erection by 10 to 100 percent depending on how hard the penis is squeezed. The second technique relies on the man gradually learning to master control over his ejaculation reflex. The therapy is divided into several phases: foreplay without intercourse; intercourse with the woman on top; and finally intercourse with the man on top. In these situations, every time the man feels he is about to ejaculate, he stops what he is doing. He starts again only when he feels he has control. It's argued that he gradually learns to sense the signals coming from his sexual organs and understands how he can control them.

Since premature ejaculation is a problem of mind over matter, the prognosis is generally very good after sex therapy, with up to 90 percent cured. What is more of a problem is a relatively small group of men who develop the condition after some years with the same partner, when there is no obvious psychological reason for the change. In these cases, it's important that they be examined by an andrologist or neurologist. It is said that one of the first signs of impotence can be premature ejaculation. The man who loses an erection rapidly after penetration has to learn how to ejaculate faster without being fully clear what the primary problem is. Certain cases of chronic prostatovesiculitis are associated with premature ejaculation because the chronic inflammation makes the nerves around the bladder neck supersensitive and causes them to fire off the reflex much faster than normal. Other more alarming reasons are spinal tumors or diseases of the nerves, such as multiple sclerosis. In cases of spina bifida, this nerve injury may have been present since the first ejaculation. Because there can be nonpsychological causes of premature ejaculation, it's vital that all cases where the condition develops late are investigated fully.

SHOOTING BLANKS

Which direction the ejaculate is sent out of the pressure chamber depends on how tightly the inner and outer valves are locked. When the inside valve is tightly locked and the outside valve is operating correctly, the ejaculate is sent in the right direction. If the outside valve is open most of the time, not enough pressure is generated in the pressure chamber and the semen just oozes out. If the inner lock is weak and the outer valve normal, the semen follows the line of least resistance and is shot into the bladder, the so-called retrograde ejaculation. In this case, the semen can be harvested from the bladder with the next urination, washed, and, if the quality is good enough, used to inseminate their partners.

Strange things also apparently happen in so-called normal males. One patient, after he had recently lost his son, began to ejaculate into his bladder each time he had sex with his wife but had a normal ejaculation when he masturbated. Because of unconscious associations, he could unknowingly open the inner valve of the pressure chamber and alter the direction of his ejaculate. Others have described men who can unconsciously divide their ejaculates into two, the first half sent out of the penis into space, the second half containing the sperm cells into the bladder. Another phenomenon is the "dry ejaculate." In this case and because of certain diseases of the nerves, the sex glands don't empty their secretions into the pressure chamber and semen can't be retrieved from the bladder with the next urination. As we will see later, both the "dry ejaculate" and retrograde ejaculation can be associated with orgasm, although its intensity can vary.

A "dry ejaculate" can also be experienced in normal men after repeated ejaculations. In actual fact, after four or five orgasms within a period of several hours, a man will usually "fire a blank," simply because his sex glands are now empty. If he continues, the next orgasm will take a lot longer and be accompanied by a feeling of "pelvic retching" and the seepage of a watery fluid that can be bloody. Casanova gloried in the self-applied nickname "Monsieur Six-fois," Mr. Six-times, because of his alleged ability to achieve six orgasms during a sexual encounter. The highest number of ejaculations that has been reliably reported by Kinsey is the eight accomplished by a thirty-nine-year-old Negro on a single occasion.

There are more obvious reasons why men suddenly begin to "shoot blanks." The most common is the mechanical deterioration of the valves of the pressure chamber after prostate operations. The most frequent prostate operation today involves removal of the center of the gland through the penis, rather like taking the core out of an apple. When this is done the man has a 40 to 50 percent chance of experiencing retrograde ejaculations. This is a lot better odds than twenty years ago, when the prostate was scooped out via an abdominal operation after which 95 percent of men woke up as retrograde ejaculators. Men who are operated on for testicular cancer often have disturbances in their ejaculation, which usually becomes retrograde, because when the lymph nodes in the pelvis are removed, the nerves controlling the inner valve of the pressure chamber are damaged. Thankfully, it is possible in some of these men to tighten up the inner valve either surgically or by using certain drugs, so the men can once again impregnate their wives by normal means. Operations on the lower part of the aorta also result in similar disturbances for the same reason. One of the drawbacks of having diabetes is that it is often associated with nerve damage that can result not only in impotence but also in ejaculation problems. In fact, a whole list of diseases can disturb or prevent the loading, firing, and direction in which the seminal bullet is ejected.

Alcohol and certain drugs including barbiturates can delay emission and ejaculation by damping the firing frequency of the spinal nerves. More serious medicines used in the treatment of blood pressure, psychosis, anxiety, and depression can cause retrograde ejaculation by interfering with the action of the nerves opening and closing the valves of the pressure chamber.

ORGASM: THE ULTIMATE GOAL

Whereas emission and ejaculation have been thought of as the mechanical side of the male climax, orgasm has been considered the sensory expression. The strange thing is that having an orgasm is an extremely difficult experience to describe and the chances are that the intensity of an orgasm differs markedly from one person to another. An expression such as "The earth moved" can be difficult for some to understand.

Orgasm has been associated with a unique state of consciousness, a loss of contact with immediate external reality. Kinsey noted that, "At orgasm some individuals may remain unconscious for a matter of seconds or even for some minutes." In one highly adventurous study, orgasm could be triggered simply by sending electrical impulses down an electrode implanted in a discrete area of the brain. In fact a "pleasure center" has been discovered in monkey brains that can be coupled up to an external switch. When animals were given the opportunity to switch the stimulus on and off themselves, by pulling a lever, they devoted all of their available time to doing so, ignoring all other activities such as eating, drinking, and sleeping. It is therefore tempting to speculate that humans may also have similar orgasm centers.

In certain forms of epilepsy associated with abnormal waves of electrical activity in the brain, the fits can trigger orgasms without ejaculation. And the analysis of brain waves of masturbating subjects showed that orgasm is associated with specific changes in the pattern of brain waves. Intriguingly, bursts of electrical activity were seen more on the right side of the brain than on the left; the reason for this is as yet unknown. But despite these findings, the majority of men are aware that during orgasm, pleasant feelings also arise further down. In women, it is associated with waves of pleasurable contractions, not only in the vagina, but also in the uterus. In fact, four seconds after a woman subjectively feels an orgasm coming on, the uterus and vagina begin to contract every 0.8 seconds, three to fifteen times on average.

In men, the pleasurable sensations of orgasm are also related to waves of activity in the accessory sex glands and along the urethra in the penis. And as in the woman, special muscle detectors have shown that orgasm starts a few seconds before ejaculation. In other words, ejaculation is not an absolute requirement for experiencing a male orgasm. They can occur quite independently of each other. We have heard earlier that there are men who are capable of multiple orgasms for every single ejaculation and this is often the case for prepubescent boys, who can experience many orgasms before the time they have begun to ejaculate. And there are many who experience ejaculations without orgasm, a situation that can also be experienced by Mr. Average from time to time. What can be said is that when emission and ejaculation are not present, the orgasm is not normal and certainly not so intense.

Over many years there have been many theories to explain the male orgasm. One of the most modern theories views it as involving many different processes. The pleasurable sensations of that part of the orgasm triggered below the belt are supposed to be related to three events: (1) the feeling of inevitability as the secretions empty the sex glands to fill and stretch the pressure chamber, (2) the release of tension as the pressure chamber deflates, and (3) the pulsating contraction of the pelvic muscles during the ejaculation. When all three are present in the proper sequence then the result is believed to be quantitatively much more satisfying than the sum of the three separate sensations. Anything that prevents any of these three events from happening or interferes with their sequence will reduce the orgasm's intensity. Of course, superimposed on these components of the orgasm are the intense relief from the general muscular and nervous tension that occurs throughout the body.

When the internal valve on the pressure chamber is damaged or weak, which is often seen in cases of retrograde ejaculation, the sensation of inevitability is reduced because the tension in the pressure chamber is lower. As a result, the release from tension is less intense, and since there is no semen in the urethra the muscle contractions at ejaculation are not so pleasing. In fact, 60 percent of retrograde ejaculators report a decrease in the intensity of orgasm compared to before. In cases of "dry emission and ejaculation," where the sex glands don't function properly, the climax is a ghostly echo of a remembered orgasm, because none of the pleasurable components are present.

It is interesting that after sex-change operations the ejaculatory orgasm does not disappear but is replaced by a climactic feeling entirely different in character from the usual orgasm. All these sensations are cloaked with the memory of past sexual experiences and modified by the social and psychological situation.

The difficulty with the scientific literature is that very little is written about changes in the intensity of the male orgasm. Sex researchers are more interested in whether it is present or not and how many are experienced. We may go through life thinking our orgasms are normal when in fact they may be the equivalent of scratching an itch for the guy next door. Certainly we are all aware that our orgasms vary from one occasion to the next with the same partner. Sexual abstinence, a long period of foreplay, or a new sexual situation are sure ways of hitting the orgasmic jackpot. This is partly because of the increased volumes of semen in the pressure chamber, but also because of the weird and wonderful tricks played on us by our senses and our gray matter, which make it one of the most deeply moving and satisfying sensory experiences for any man.

9 APHRODISIACS: THE CHEMISTRY OF LOVE

Most men, at one time or another, have wished for a sure-fire pill that would drive a girl mad with lust or passion and for a potion to turn them into super studs—so potent, so virile that she would never look at another guy. These are not new dreams. The idea of a love potion can be traced far back into the mists of time and it was the man more often than the woman who placed orders for these concoctions with the local witch or apothecary. Stories abound in ancient literature, such as the *Arabian Nights,* of potions "to harden the eggs and thicken the sap when it becomes too thin."

Since the days of alchemy and presumably in response to an increasing demand from a frustrated male public, wise men and women, scientists, and quacks have brewed all manner of strange love potions or aphrodisiacs (from Aphrodite, the Greek goddess of love) to lure and to impress unsuspecting members of the fair sex. Most of them were magical, belonging to the world of wish fulfillment rather than to the real world. Other concoctions, although few in number, undoubtedly had genuine effects on the sex lives of our forefathers, secrets that are only now being disclosed by modern science.

THE FOODS OF LOVE

It is not surprising that the first aphrodisiacs were based on plants and foodstuffs, and it can't have been a coincidence that the majority of them in their natural state closely resembled the male or female sexual organs or shared the same perfume as the sex secretions. When the ancient Greeks and Romans wanted to spice up their sex lives, they drank a couple of drams of a stuff called Satyrion (from the Greek word Satyr, a god indulging in sexual excesses), which was made from a kind of orchid with bulbs shaped like human testicles. It is said that "Hercules, receiving the beverage from Thespius, deflowered the fifty daughters of his hostess in one night." And even in the 1960s, extracts of Satyrion were being sold by London's West End chemists to wide-eyed wishful thinkers.

The mandrake was another ancient aphrodisiacal plant, whose root had a human form, right down to the penis. It was said that when a person was hanged he ejaculated and that the mandrake sprang out from the earth where the semen fell. In the Middle Ages, eating a plate full of onions was a sure way of prolonging an erection and increasing your sperm count, a property shared by other testicle-sized vegetables such as garlic, radishes, and turnips. Of course, cucumbers and leeks could do little for a man's fertility, but were dynamite for a sagging erection. Fruits with lots of seeds like the pomegranate or fig were recommended for those wanting plenty of babies. And the fact that the fig resembled the female sex organs also must have added a little spice to the sex act when the family was being planned.

It was often the case that when new foods were introduced into a country they often were regarded for a short time as an aphrodisiac. Chocolate and the potato had their days, and the old Middle Ages name for the tomato was love apple. The association between the apple and the Garden of Eden explains why, for a period in Europe, women were presented with a Granny Smith instead of a box of

After Eight mints. Others were given presents of pears, the favorite fruit of the goddess Venus, in the hope that one bite would make a woman a sex slave. Of course it can't have taken too long before aspiring Valentinos were getting sick of daily onions, leeks, and turnips without the desired effects, and began to turn to more exotic, harder-to-get potions, but still with a clear symbolic component—such as rhino horn rissoles and powdered reindeer antler.

Others went directly to the source and went on a diet of stewed sex organs—bull and dog testicles, dried animal dongs, and even human and bull semen. The latter was considered a great turn-on for breaking down the resistance of reluctant women. How they managed to persuade them to drink it is still a well-kept secret! Finally, we come to one of the most famous aphrodisiacs of all—the humble oyster, the smell of which is said by some to be like the human ejaculate. Others have described the experience of eating oysters to be "like having angels copulate on the tongue."

> A young bride feeds her husband oysters on their wedding night but later complains they were not satisfactory, "I fed him a dozen but only nine of them worked!"

A recent scientific publication that raised a few eyebrows confirmed that oysters do indeed increase potency, apparently because of their high content of zinc, believed by some zealots to work wonders with the male sex organ. The list of foods claimed to act as aphrodisiacs is endless and illustrates the desperate nature of the quest for love stimulants.

HOW APHRODISIACS REALLY WORK

In folklore the original definition of an aphrodisiac was a potion or spell used to transform a reluctant damsel into a raving nymphomaniac who only had eyes for you. Today an aphrodisiac has four scientific meanings: an activator, one which increases the desire to have sex usually by removing one's inhibitions; a rejuvenator, an elixir that gave old men the sexiness of their youth; a prolonger or sustainer of sexual performance, a substance that could turn a hopeless lover into an inexhaustible stud; and a hedonic amplifier, something that heightens the senses in connection with sex and intensifies orgasm. Do such substances really exist today? Let's take a look at the facts.

APHRODISIACS THAT INCREASE DESIRE

The desire to have sex comes from one of the most primitive areas of the human brain—the limbic system. The nerve pathways to and from this sex center are like a telephone exchange system with special chemicals performing the task of transmitting electrical messages between the different nerves. In general, completion of the circuits that arouse somebody depends on a chemical called dopamine. The circuits of frigidity are controlled by serotonin. Anything that increases the amount of dopamine or turns off the supply of serotonin in our brains will theoretically increase sexual desire. Anything doing the opposite can turn us into nuns and monks. Many so-called modern aphrodisiacs work by altering the balance of these chemicals in the brain. Some of the medicines used in psychiatry that often have the side effect of reducing sexual desire or potency do so by reducing the dopamine levels. In contrast, L-dopa, a medicine used in the treatment of a nerve disorder called Parkinson's disease, was once acclaimed as an aphrodisiac because it not only kept the disorder under control, but also made the elderly patients so horny that nurses had to do their rounds in twos for fear of having their bottoms pinched.

It is also interesting that three street drugs believed to stimulate the desire to have sex—cocaine, amphetamines, and LSD—all block serotonin in the brain and increase the levels of dopamine. The problem with amphetamines is that for some reason, they also increase the desire to indulge in bizarre sexual behavior. One woman developed a craving to be licked by dogs and a man developed pedophilic tendencies under the influence of amphetamines. Even more horrifying is the condition associated with amphetamine abuse, "shriveled penis syndrome," which leaves little to the imagination.

Because of the way it stimulates sexual desire in both sexes, the male hormone, testosterone, has been acclaimed by some to be the only true aphrodisiac. Any bodybuilder can attest that the synthetic male hormone in anabolic steroids can make a man lustful. Indeed, scientists have shown that testosterone acts like a mind-stimulating drug by altering the levels of the nerve chemicals in the sex centers of the brain.

In English folklore, oats, especially the wild variety, often pop up in connection with sexual desire. "Feeling your oats" or "sowing your wild oats" are euphemisms for lustfulness and sexual promiscuity. It is interesting in this respect, that there is an herbal mixture currently being patented as an aphrodisiac that is composed of nothing more than oats, vitamin C, and nettle extract and is guaranteed to increase sex desire. A series of scientific studies has shown that after eating this mixture there is an increase in the levels of biologically active male hormone in the blood. Here then is a perfect example of how dangerous it is to scoff at the historical aphrodisiacs, no matter how mind boggling and farfetched they may be!

Most of us go around inhibiting the animal instincts that tell us to make passionate love with any or all of the members of the opposite sex we meet. Presumably we do this by holding a tight rein on our dopamine levels. Any drug or chemical that can remove these inhibitions and loosen the restraint on our sex centers can theoretically act like an aphrodisiac and make horny devils of us all. Alcohol is regarded as the classical remover of sexual inhibitions. Many of us have heard of the sexual orgies associated with the festivals of Bacchus (the God of Drink) in ancient Rome. And the saying that "Candy is dandy but liquor is quicker" reminds us of the general belief that alcohol is much quicker at getting women in bed than buying them presents. Cannabis, like alcohol, also increases the likelihood of sex by removing inhibitions and has been used for hundreds of years in the Far East for this purpose. However, like alcohol, the effects of smoking hashish are very dose-dependent—too much, too frequently has an opposite effect and suppresses the sex drive. Their effects are also dependent on the social context. Smoking cannabis at a football game is not likely to make you want to make love to the referee! So any substance that removes our natural inhibitions—and there are many—can theoretically qualify as an aphrodisiac.

APHRODISIACS THAT AMPLIFY OR PROLONG SEXUAL PERFORMANCE

For thousands of years, man has used hallucinogenic drugs made from plants and mushrooms to enhance and amplify the sensory signals associated with the sexual act and to intensify orgasm. Nutmeg is an example of a spice believed to contain such hallucinogens; in the Middle Ages it was recommended as an aphrodisiac. Today, street drugs have replaced these natural sources. In studies by the famous sexologists Masters and Johnson, 75 percent of men and women who regularly smoked cannabis did so because it made sex better, not because it made them relax, but because it also increased the sense of touch and in 60 percent of men increased the intensity of orgasm. Cocaine is called by addicts the champagne of sex drugs, not only because it affects sexual desire by altering the levels of the brain chemicals in the sex centers, but also because it increases the sensitivity of the sex organs once sex has started.

Angel dust, mescaline, and LSD are extremely dangerous

street drugs reported by addicts to amplify the feelings of touch during sex. The problem with these "hedonic amplifiers" when it comes to sex is the fine line between a good and bad trip, which is related to dose, timing, the individual, and the social context. Not only that, if you do manage to feel any benefit, it's difficult to go back to "boring sex" afterwards, creating the need to use the stuff regularly for sexual satisfaction.

Two drugs that came into popular use as narcotic aphrodisiacs in the 1960s were Quaaludes and poppers or amyl nitrate. Amyl nitrate prolonged the perception of orgasm if sniffed just before. It worked by relaxing smooth muscle and increasing blood flow through the sexual organs. Gay men made use of its muscle-relaxing effect by sniffing it before anal sex. The problem was that if your sniff timing was a little off, instead of having an orgasm that blew your mind you ended up with a shriveled penis.

SUPER STUD FOR A DAY

Since the beginnings of civilization, men have searched for a miracle substance that could transform the impotent, the premature ejaculators, and any below-average lovers into professional studs with metal-hard, semipermanent erections capable of bringing tears of joy to a woman's eyes. In fact, the prototypes must have brought tears of agony to the user's eyes. The most notorious was Spanish fly, a powder made by grinding the dried bodies of a beetle called cantharis. One spoonful of the stuff caused a stinging and burning sensation in the kidneys and urinal passage and vagina associated with pooling of blood in the pelvis. The result was an erection or an itchy vagina that you had an irresistible urge to scratch, preferably through intercourse. In 1954, two London office girls were unwittingly given Spanish fly mixed with candy and died a few hours later in agony. Ginseng root also has a mild irritant effect on the urinary system causing an itching that also has been said to increase the desire to have sex. Similar effects to those brought on by Spanish fly and ginseng can be achieved by rubbing lotions of pepper, ginger, or mustard directly on the penis.

One of the few traditional aphrodisiacs with an effect on erection that has been verified by scientists is yohimbine, an extract from the bark of a West African tree. This substance has been shown to have a direct effect on the spongy tissue of the penis and is becoming increasingly used in the treatment of impotence. Because it has been around for a long, long time, jokes abound about its effects on the erection:

> An elderly gentleman who is dining with a sweet young girl slips the headwaiter a packet of yohimbine pills and tells him to put one in the soup. The dinner is delayed and when the man complains, the waiter replies "Sorry, sir, but we are still waiting for the noodles to lie down."

Only in the last ten years have substances become available that satisfy the original requirements of a pure aphrodisiac in causing an erection that can be sustained for hours despite ejaculation. These drugs, like papaverine, which are also being used in the treatment of impotence, belong to a family of drugs that can be injected directly into the penis. The results are an erection that can last from two to twenty hours—not bad for someone previously impotent! Such medicines combined with testosterone are probably the closest we will ever come to a male elixir of youth, a rejuvenator of lost sexual powers.

A perusal through the majority of international men's magazines reminds us of today's million-dollar market for aphrodisiacs. Millions of dollars are spent every year by men wanting to feel their effects. The majority are useless, containing nothing more than vitamins and a dash of ginseng. Most rely on a placebo effect and a great deal of erotic fantasy. Some are even cheeky enough to assume the public's ignorance by advertising aphrodisiacs called Spanish Fly Placebo—in other words sugar pills called Spanish fly. However, as any poet would attest, the electricity between two people in love is the greatest aphrodisiac of all and as long as that remains pure and lasting, the use of love potions and drugs perverts the meaning of that love.

10 SEMEN: NATURE'S LIQUID OF LIFE

Our first experience of life's liquid can frighten, embarrass, or even shock. Nobody prepares you. Puberty is well on its way; a strange, pleasant feeling wakes you from a dream; you feel wet down there. No, you haven't suddenly become incontinent, it's your first wet dream . . . an uncontrollable ejaculation . . . nature's way of relieving the pressure fueled by the male hormone testosterone . . . sex glands bursting with sex fluids, ready to erupt with an erotic thought, a glimpse of panties, a flash of milky breast. A milestone in your life has just passed. But innocent, uncontrollable wet dreams are soon replaced by the carnal thrills of masturbation. Life's liquid is suddenly not a precious bodily fluid to be preserved. It becomes irreverently disseminated with gusto—twice a day and three times on Sundays! No one contemplates the awesome possibility that it is in limited supply.

Small practical problems arise for our young onanist—tell-tale stains on bedsheets that miraculously can now stand up for themselves: guilt . . . damnable evidence of a shameful act, a feeling of doing something one shouldn't. Rumors of celestial punishment abound—hairy palms, blindness, and withered sexual organs—but then you discover that there are millions of spotty-faced teenagers enthusiastically regularly emptying their glands without going blind, deaf, or insane. Why the guilt and where did all those dreadful stories come from?

A little boy was caught in the act of masturbating in the local church by the vicar. "Can't you save all that until you're married?" roared the vicar angrily. The boy scurried off in a hurry. Twenty years go by and the same boy now stands in front of the same vicar in a marriage ceremony. "Do you remember me, father?" "No, my son," replies the priest. The boy reminds him of the episode in the church. "And do you remember that you told me to save it until I got married?" "Yes." "Well, I've saved six and a half liters of the stuff. What do you want me to do with it?"

IS IT WORTH BRAIN DAMAGE?

The know-alls of ancient times actually believed that every time you had an ejaculation you lost a small amount of your brain. They called semen *cerebri stillicidium*, which, roughly translated, means distillate of brains. Camus, a great thinker who presumably had never lost a drop of gray matter, announced that semen was microscopic "brains" that came directly from the "great brain." Even Hippocrates thought of semen as a fermentation carried by the spinal cord to the sex organs. Aurelius Celsus must have precipitated an international depression when he told a horrified world that the loss of semen caused wasting of the spinal cord. Hippocrates must have agreed with him because he invented a name for it—*tabes dorsalis*—spinal consumption caused by too many ejaculations. These ancient beliefs must have stopped a lot of men from going around with their hands in their pockets and were almost certainly responsible for the terror campaigns of the nineteenth century during which learned men became preoccupied with the evils of ejaculation. The superstition that spilling salt causes bad luck is believed to symbolize the awful consequences of spilling one's seed. Presumably it's easier to throw salt over your shoulder than a handful of semen.

In 1845, a leading European doctor wrote that too many wet dreams and too much masturbation caused by reading dirty books and having dirty thoughts "keeps up a constant irritation to the point that seminal secretions become chronic," in other words the poor wretch started leaking semen. "Before too long . . . his body becomes debilitated, his sexual organs impotent and both the generative fluids and the vital forces of the body drain to such an alarming degree that the victim all too often succumbed to consumption, epilepsy, insanity, or an early grave." One popular nineteenth-century sex manual wrote that Samson's loss of strength was due not to his loss of hair but to the loss of semen caused by all his dirty thoughts about Delilah. Too much sex and loss of semen was also to blame when Calhoun in 1858 wrote, "The man generally suffers more than women, because women do not exhaust themselves as men do and preserve their health better."

Bartholow writing in 1866 suspected that prolonged sitting in school caused an unhealthy accumulation of blood below the belt and an unnatural development of the genitals, which in turn encouraged seminal leakage. Some such as Bigelow began to shake a finger and warn that untreated chronic loss of sperm caused weakness of the mind, dullness, listlessness, shadowy dreams instead of intellectual labor, increasingly poor respiration, and an irregular heart beat. Practitioners later developed a pale complexion, dull pains in the loins, constipation, watery eyes, loss of memory, shrinkage of the sex organs, and pendulous testicles. Later stages were thought to bring catalepsy, epilepsy, mania, or some other disease of the nervous system, relieved only by a premature death.

Having scared the wits out of the adolescent male population with detailed accounts of how their brains would rot and how their sex organs would wither and fall off, the medical experts of the nineteenth century recommended ways by which parents could staunch the rivers of semen before it was too late. The simplest course was to tie the unfortunate child's hands to the bedpost or make him wear a towel around his waist with a large knot in it to stop him from lying on his back. A little more sophisticated was an arrangement with an electric bell that burst into life when the penis of our sleeping would-be wet dreamer became erect and completed an electric circuit. A sadistic turn was the development of a metal penis ring with spikes turned inwards, designed to make a sieve out of a twitching tumescent organ. Some recommended the use of a leather thong wrapped around the penis that tightened and caused excruciating pain. "Rather like stopping a man from throwing up by squeezing his throat," was the comment of one of its opponents.

Armand Trousseau around the early 1800s brought new meaning to the adage "go to work on an egg" when he recommended putting a wooden egg into the rectum, large enough to press on the prostate gland and send semen the wrong way into the bladder. Pretty soon these eggs became popular over much of Europe, not only wooden but also metal and hand-painted porcelain ones—the ideal Christmas gift for anybody looking suspiciously off color. An interesting recommendation was the use of lead bed sheets, so heavy that it was almost impossible to raise your elbows and get into a proper rhythm. Even drugs such as quinine, digitalis, cannabis, opium, and potassium bromide were forced down young gullets. Injections of tepid water into the rectum, electromagnetism, bloodletting, and, horror of horrors, even castration were also seriously discussed as ways of avoiding a premature death.

As late as 1876 a book was published that described semen as not only the best-quality nerve juice but also as equivalent to forty times its weight in blood. The book recommended several ways of avoiding springing a seminal leak: avoid oysters; take plenty of cold baths; do not attend intimate dinners; drink no alcohol; do not talk to questionable women; and last but not least don't go to sleep with the rays of the moon falling on you!

Happily for all the advocates of seminal liberation in the twentieth century, schools of thought evolved in these dark ages stating that wet dreams and other seminal leakages were as natural as menstruation and a lot more fun, "a periodic relief for frustrated organs." At last sanity had prevailed and spotty schoolboys could once again walk openly with their hands in the holes in their pockets.

A little boy is sitting in a tree, tugging his tool like a steam engine. A little old lady comes along and stops to glare up at him.

"Do you realize, young man," she says, "that by spilling your seed you could be wasting the life of a great statesman, a brilliant artist, or even a great religious leader? Heaven knows what marvellous potential you are destroying!"

The boy is impressed but it's too late to stop. He comes and a large blob of semen flies through the air, hits a branch, drips to a leaf, and bounces from one leaf to another finally spinning down to land at her feet.

"I guess you're right," he says. "There goes an Olympic gymnast!"

SEMINAL VOLUME

A quick perusal through the porno literature would give the average man a king-size inferiority complex. "He exploded in hot gushing torrents of spunk," "I filled her to the brim with my love cream," "She drowned in liters of cum." It all seems a little exaggerated when one realizes that the average ejaculate would fill a dessert spoon—about .2 cubic inches—hardly enough to drown in. Surely there are men who could fill an egg cup with each ejaculation, but these are rare, and their wives would attest that such a talent is not an advantage when the women stand up. The stallion and boar top the animal league for ejaculates, with discharges of up to one-third and one-half of a liter, respectively. This may explain why it is not uncommon for a boar to fall asleep on the sow's back after he has erupted, with of course a smile on its face.

The human sex glands have little storage capacity and are soon emptied after repeated ejaculations. In a group of students paid to masturbate every eight hours for two days, the average semen volume decreased by 50 percent with every ejaculate until after two days there were only bubbles. It took three days of complete abstinence before they could fill dessert spoons again.

On the other hand, semen is also produced by nerves during the excitement phase of the sexual act; the longer the period of heavy kissing and petting, the more intense the activity of the nerves and the larger the semen volume. This explains why an ejaculate after intercourse is at least 20 percent larger than one produced through masturbation, even by someone with a vivid imagination. And several animal studies have indicated that the sex glands of frequent ejaculators are larger than those of their celibate brothers, indicating that our organs can compensate for increased demands. But what use is cum besides being associated with a pleasant sensation?

THE COMPOSITION OF SEMEN

When man was a small jelly creature floating around in the primordial sea, it's highly unlikely that his orgasms were worth writing home about. Sperms were hiccuped out into the surrounding water and had to swim towards the eggs, attracted to them by underwater perfumes. When we evolved to the land we had to create our own bit of sea so that the journey to the egg could continue. But semen is far more than a mobile swimming pool. It is a soup containing a myriad of enigmatic substances designed to aid the sperm cells on the first part of their journey. There is a sugar for topping up the sperm's energy reserves, an antibiotic to prevent the growth of unwanted bacteria, a substance that helps the sperm sneak past the police cells of the vagina on the lookout for foreign-looking cells, chemicals to change the acid environment of the vagina into a more hospitable place for sperm, and other chemicals that somehow switch on delicate chemical processes in the sperm so that by the time it reaches the egg it's ripe for penetration. In fact there are hundreds of substances in this gonadal gazpacho whose presence we know about but whose function has still to be learned. Semen is a witch's brew whose secrets will remain hidden for many decades.

HOW SEMEN IS PRODUCED

Egyptians believed that semen circulated around the body like blood; I have mentioned earlier that many later peoples believed that it came from the nervous system. Today we know that seminal fluid is a cocktail produced mainly by two of the sex glands—a little less than half from the prostate gland and more than half from the two seminal vesicles. These two glands complement each other in an impressive way. Almost immediately after semen emerges from the penis, it clumps due to a chemical reaction between the two types of secretions. A net of proteins forms to imprison the sperm cells. After about twenty minutes at room temperature, but faster in the warmer vagina, this clump magically liquefies because chemical scissors produced in the prostate gland begin to snip away at the net and cut it into smaller and smaller fragments. The clump finally becomes liquid, releasing the sperm, which, with explosive speed, swim into the cervix leaving the seminal fluid behind.

It's not often realized that it's only the sperm cells, equivalent in total volume to the head of a matchstick, that actually leave the vagina. The rest gradually soaks through the vaginal wall. Why does semen come out in a clump and then gradually become liquid? Some have said that it makes the ejaculate like a bullet and gives it better velocity. It also concentrates it in one place. But the most important reason is probably to keep the sperm in contact with these fluids a short time so they have a chance to work their chemical miracles. It takes time for the fluids to make the vagina more hospitable before you allow the sperm cells to take the plunge. Of course some sperm will escape relatively quickly and just three minutes after ejaculation some are already on their way into the cervix. But these are in the minority.

Only 10 percent of the semen volume, that containing the sperm cells, actually comes from the testicles. This is why sterilized men, who have knots tied in the tubes from their testicles, don't notice any difference in the volume of their ejaculate. What is difficult to understand is that semen actually comes out of the body in a train of different secretions following after each other. First is the prostate fluid, which is thin and watery, then comes the sperm from the testicles, followed by the fluid from the seminal vesicles, which is thicker and creamy. A few seconds after mixing, the semen clump forms. It is for this reason that trying to prevent pregnancy by withdrawing the penis before orgasm can be a risky business. The first half of the ejaculate often comes before orgasm and it is this watery fraction, which does not look white and creamy enough to be real semen, that often contains the highest number of sperm.

THE LUBRICATING FLUID

The prostate gland and the seminal vesicles are the two most important sex glands, but there are several others that help make up the total ejaculate. During petting, nervous impulses are sent to two small pea-sized glands at the base of the penis called Cowper's glands. Anticipating an imminent ejaculation, these glands squeeze out a thick oily substance that spreads down the tube in the penis covering the inside of the urethra. Why? Maybe to reduce friction so that the ejaculate can skate along at high speed. It may also help to neutralize any urine residues that might be harmful to the delicate sperm. Usually only two to three drops but sometimes more is produced, and this substance can be seen if the penis is squeezed during the excitement phase.

SEMINAL FINGERPRINTS

As all adolescent boys would agree, seminal stains are not the easiest things to hide or get rid of. It arouses a lot of suspicion when a son insists that he's going to help his mother more around the house and start by washing his pajamas and bedsheets. The smell of semen is another give-away because it is very characteristic. Some say that the closest to it in nature is something called oil of wintergreen. The smell is due to a chemical called spermine, spewed out of the prostate gland in such quantities that it crystalizes during drying. These very special crystals were used for many years as a forensic test for semen. Today the tests are much more complicated but still rely on detecting the presence of one of the products of the sex glands. If enough sperm cells can be harvested, the use of the new gene technology enables the seminal detectives to obtain a genetic fingerprint of the culprit, almost as good as giving the police a Polaroid snapshot!

Semen really is nature's water of life because it contains and protects those microscopic cells that participate in the creation of life—a highly complex cocktail and our own piece of primordial sea. An average male will ejaculate thirty to fifty quarts between the ages of fifteen and sixty, containing 350 to 500 billion sperm cells. Whole swimming pools of semen are produced every day on a worldwide basis. Those old nineteenth-century physicians must be turning in their graves!

MALE

SEXUAL

HEALTH

AND

SEXUAL

DYSFUNCTION

11 THE CAUSES OF IMPOTENCE

I am getting old and have almost reached my barrier, What used to be my magic wand is now my water carrier!

I look back to the beautiful time when all joints were flexible, but one.
But those times are over and all the joints become stiff except one.

Impotence. It is a word to send shudders down the mightiest of male organs . . . a word striking at the very soul of maleness . . . a word beyond the sexual, a word synonymous with ineptitude, weakness, the state of being useless. It is a powerful word never to be uttered lightly, not even in jest, because once voiced, no matter how unjustified, the thought can reverberate around the cerebral circuits and become a reality. Yes, as we will see, the brain can play funny tricks when it involves the penis.

THE SYMBOLIC IMPORTANCE OF AN ERECTION

Getting an erection is the essence of male dominance and nowhere do we see it better than in our monkey cousins. Many a monkey demonstrates dominance by simply sticking his swollen penis into the face of his would-be competitors.

It can't have taken too long before our primitive ancestors got fed up with flashing themselves every time a stranger approached. Instead they took the easy way out and stooped to deception. The jungle men of Papua New Guinea hide their penises in arm-long penis tubes, and tribes in the New Hebrides pack their organs in banana leaves to fool the opposition, or at least keep them guessing! In Europe in the Middle Ages the gentry hid their penises in a padded extension of their clothes called a codpiece, which gave the impression of a mighty erection lurking inside. Students of human behavior tell us that the irate driver who gives the finger-up sign when you try to remind him that the traffic lights have changed is, believe it or not, symbolically flashing an erect penis to express his disdain. In fact, this phallic signal (and the bent-arm gesture) go back almost two thousand years and probably saved us the trouble of dropping our trousers when it was inconvenient.

Body watchers also tell us that the sure way of recognizing the self-certain dominant male is to note the way he sits: lounging with his legs spread apart, subconsciously or consciously exposing his genitals to his competitors and potential conquests. Contrast this to the reserved quiet man with his knees held tightly together.

THE STATISTICS ON IMPOTENCE

Men can be inflicted with the horrors of impotence at any age. However, generally it is associated with the more elderly members of our sex. At age fifty-five, 8 percent of healthy men suffer from it; at age sixty-five, 25 percent; at age seventy-five, 55 percent; and at age eighty, as many as 75 percent have experienced the frustration of impotence. The wealth of jokes on impotence associated with old age testifies to the need for laughing at other men's problems while removing the attention from one's own. The following joke illustrates how far some men can go in denying a fact of life:

> An elderly man goes to the doctor and says he has a question to ask. He proceeds to tell the doctor that in his youth he could get an erection so hard that it was like an iron bar; he could not push it down with both hands. "In all of my sexual encounters it was always the same, I could not push it down with two hands. But in the last few years, I can push it down not only with two hands but even with one. Doc, do you think I'm getting stronger?"

THE CAUSES OF IMPOTENCE

Primitive man looking down on a limp organ had no possibilities of writing to Dr. Ruth for advice. He took the easy way out and blamed it on the gods. Even the Bible (Genesis 20) blames impotence on a divine curse. But by the Middle Ages it was witchcraft and sorcery that were the scapegoats, and an effective treatment was burning the local witch. But when there were no more witches to kick around, the wise urologists of the day had to focus on the person himself. "Too much masturbation!" cried the moralists. "Sexual excess!" cried the church. The bewildered looked down on their limp organs and wondered whether they had worn them out. Even as late as 1961, supposed experts were saying masturbation could cause impotence.

STATUS, STRESS, AND IMPOTENCE

Several writers have emphasized the inextricably close connection between the feeling of status and an ability to perform well in bed. Henry Kissinger once said that the possession of power is the greatest aphrodisiac. In groups of chimpanzees, the dominant male (or his erection) appears to block the sex drive of the other males as long as he is running the show, causing their own tools to wilt. As many psychologists would confirm, one of the first body organs to be adversely affected by stress and overwork is the one between the thighs. Maybe deep within the recesses of our minds, tucked away in a nerve cell somewhere in a primitive part of our gray matter, there are preprogramed associations that affect our image of being male. Anything that distorts that image—a sexually frustrated wife, setbacks at work, losing status in the family—may influence our libido and potency to an alarming degree. With the rise of feminism many men prophesized the end of civilization as we then knew it. Books were written forecasting epidemics of impotence as women gradually took more and more control in the sexual act, taking away the male initiative and his hunting instinct.

FETISHES AND IMPOTENCE

The subconscious plays a large part when a particular fetish leads to selective impotence. There are an unfortunate few who can get an erection only with a ninety-pound ballerina dancing on their chests; the fetishist who is potent only if his partner is dressed up as a nun, or a stripper, or a schoolteacher. The list is endless and is a beautiful illustration of how nerves can play funny tricks—the result of associations that go back to a hidden childhood memory, a forgotten episode, a suppressed desire. There are men who have problems with extramarital sex because of unconscious feelings of guilt.

CHOLESTEROL, CIRCULATION, AND IMPOTENCE

When a man gets excited he has to pump twenty times more blood than normal through his limp organ to get it to stand to attention. One of the problems of getting older is that the blood vessels carrying blood to the various organs often get partly blocked with cholesterol, and the penis is no exception. The result is that getting an erection is as difficult as pumping up the Hindenburg through a straw! One frustrating consequence of this condition is that some men, having achieved an admirable erection, see it fall to half mast when they begin to have intercourse. The reason is that when our hero begins to get into a rhythm, his buttock muscles begin to demand more blood and "steal" it from the penis, whose blood supply is already reduced to a trickle because of clogged pipes. Not only that, the hydraulic system of the penis can work properly only if the veins carrying blood from the erect penis can be clamped shut at the right moment. Try pumping up a bicycle tire with a puncture! Unfortunately, these veins also can become leaky with age and this can explain why some men have difficulties in keeping their erection hard enough to put it to use. In general, we can reckon that these circulatory problems are major causes of impotence in about 30 to 40 percent of the cases. In younger men, circulatory problems are more likely due to a congenital abnormality of the blood vessels or the result of an injury.

NERVES AND IMPOTENCE

As mentioned earlier, erection is dependent on electrical signals bombarding the spongy tissue of the penis and causing it to expand. There are many forms of illness that cause permanent damage to these electrical circuits and "unplug" the penis from the brain centers. Men with diabetes are particularly prone to this problem; in fact, 50 to 70 percent of men with diabetes (2.5 million men in the United States) suffer from impotence. This is partly because of this type of nerve injury, but is also due in part to disturbances in their metabolism, as they have a greater tendency to develop clogged arteries than other men. Often impotence can be the first sign of diabetes, but there are other conditions that can cause impotence—from a prolapsed disc to various operations of the pelvic organs, from special nerve diseases such as multiple sclerosis to injury caused by accidents. In fact, electrical failure can alone explain erection problems in about one-third of the cases. In this connection, professional cyclists can have temporary problems with their potency after a long race, partly because of pressure on the erection nerves and partly because of a temporary rearrangement in pelvic plumbing.

TESTOSTERONE AND IMPOTENCE

The male hormone, testosterone, is admittedly the fuel that keeps the fires of sex burning. However, it's generally believed that there has to be a drastic reduction in the amount circulating in the blood before the erection is affected. In fact, several studies have shown that a relatively large number of men are still sexually active two years after castration. Today, depending on whom you ask, the number of men whose impotence is the result of problems with their hormones varies between 5 and 20 percent with the former being more likely.

ALCOHOL, NICOTINE, AND IMPOTENCE

Although it's often not the main cause of impotence, a man's life-style can often make matters worse. Smoking is a notorious example. Researchers have seen that smoking two high-nicotine cigarettes immediately before viewing a porno film reduces the size of the erection compared to men smoking low-nicotine cigarettes or chewing on a candy bar. Smoking also interferes with the chemical erection that doctors can now produce by injecting drugs directly in the penis. It therefore can't come as much of a surprise that doctors have discovered that impotent men usually smoke much more than the general population. Nicotine, it seems, can play havoc with the delicate chemical balance in the sponge tissue of the penis.

In *Macbeth*, Shakespeare wrote of alcohol, "It provokes

the desire, but it takes away the performance." Alcohol in small amounts reduces anxiety, lowers inhibitions, and frees erotic desire. It also dilates the blood vessels, bringing warm sensations to all parts of the body including the penis. Unfortunately it doesn't take much more of the demon drink before the penis deteriorates in terms of performance. Studies involving measurements of erection size and vaginal contractions in test subjects who were given alcohol and then shown erotic films clearly showed that it reduced the sexual response. In fact, Masters and Johnson, in their famous series of sex studies, found that most men experience their first failed erection while under the influence of alcohol, and among men in their late forties and early fifties, impotence is "more highly associated with excessive alcohol consumption than with any other single factor."

MEDICATION AND IMPOTENCE

Almost a third of men who are regularly in and out of the hospital because of a medical problem suffer from impotence. In many cases the cause can lie in the medicines they take—medicine for blood pressure, stomach ulcers, epilepsy—the list is long. In fact, 16 of the top 200 medicines in the United States are known to interfere with erection. It is often a problem of priorities, but usually the patient is the last to know and seldom given the choice by his doctor.

IS IT ALL IN THE MIND?

Thirty years ago, Masters and Johnson, like Freud, announced that in the vast majority of cases, impotence had little to do with the hydraulic machinery, but more to do with the guy pushing the buttons. Today, we know better and can calculate that in only 10 percent of cases is impotence a purely psychological problem. Of course, once the erection begins to sag for other reasons, the fear of impotence is enough to deliver the *coup de grâce*. But there is little point in seeking psychiatric help before the various physical causes are ruled out.

A fact of life is that the vast majority of men will sooner or later experience some degree of impotence. Fortunately, as we will soon appreciate, we are living in a time when new medical discoveries can help men reach erection whether the penis wants to or not. Then we can get him to perform even when the glint has left his eye.

12 GETTING TREATMENT FOR IMPOTENCE

Now King David was old and stricken in years and they covered him with clothes but he gat no heat. Wherefore his servants said unto him, "Let there be sought for my lord the king a young virgin: and let her stand before the king, and let her cherish him, and let her lie in thy bosom, that my lord the king may get heat" (I Kings 1:1–2).

It seems that the Jews had a novel way of dealing with the problem of impotence in ancient times. However, the chances that health insurance would cover the expenses of similar treatment today is doubtful, especially in view of the extreme scarcity of suitable virgins. Certainly, this must be one of the simplest ways of finding out whether the penis is just sleeping or departed this life for good. A less popular form of stimulating potency must have been that reported to have been used by the Amazons, the ancient tribe of female warriors, who took male prisoners not only to work as slaves but also to satisfy their sexual demands. They broke or amputated the arms or legs of their captives because they believed that "the genital member was strengthened by deprivation of one of the extremities." The majority of men would presumably prefer the Jewish solution to the problem.

For modern man the first challenge is recognizing that he has a problem. After fruitless months of coaxing, prodding, and pleading with the penis to do its stuff, and faced with possible divorce proceedings, he decides to make the long journey to the doctor's office . . . alone—with the words still ringing in his ears, "Come back with an erection or else!"

THE INITIAL DOCTOR'S VISIT

A young man coming to the doctor is unlikely to have the same cause of impotence as an older man unless he has been so sexually active that he has prematurely worn out his organ, and it's therefore only natural that the questions asked by the doctor in his search for the cause will be different. Nevertheless, in both cases the question foremost in the doctor's mind is the same: "Is the cause between the ears or below the belt?" The doctor may ask, "Can you masturbate with a stiff penis?" "Do you sometimes wake up with a stiff penis?" "Do you have impotence only in specific situations (such as with your wife)?" A nod of the head to one or all of these questions, especially in a younger man, will at least suggest that the hydraulic system is in working order and that the problem may be psychological.

On the other hand, if the patient says that it takes a long time to get an erection or that he loses his erections before ejaculation, it could indicate a circulatory problem, either clogged or leaky blood vessels or a bit of both. "Do you still have the desire for sex?" is an important question, as is whether he shaves less than he did before or whether he has symptoms like hot flushes, which could suggest that the man is going through a male menopause and simply needs a shot of male hormone to bring the penis back to life. The doctor can also give sound advice to men smoking high-nicotine cigarettes, abusing alcohol, sniffing cocaine, mainlining heroin, or indulging in all four at the same time:

Kick the habit unless you want to ruin your sex life! It's more difficult when it comes to men taking large quantities of certain medicines such as heart or ulcer tablets whose side effects can be impotence. Either alternative medicines have to be tried or the doctor has to juggle with the dose so that a compromise can be reached between the penis and the other vital organs. The detective work at the first consulation is vital for the outcome, and no stone must be left unturned. And no consultation at the doctor's office would be complete before a blood and urine analysis is done. The blood is tested in some cases to check whether there is enough male hormone present, and the urine is analyzed to check for sugar, just in case the impotence is the first sign of diabetes.

EXAMINATION OF THE PENIS ITSELF

Having ruled out a number of possible causes for the erection problem, your doctor will most likely want to examine the penis itself, for several reasons. The appearance of the penis and testicles may suggest a lack of male hormone, a situation that is becoming increasingly easier to correct. More important, an examination provides an opportunity for the doctor to check the penis's pulse and to check its blood pressure. The blood pressure is measured by using a miniature version of the cuff normally used around the arm to measure blood pressure at the doctor's office. Ideally both pressures should be compared—when the arm pressure approaches double the pressure in the penis, it suggests that the arteries delivering blood to the penis need unclogging. Often the man has other symptoms that suggest clogged arteries are a systemic problem and not just a problem of the penis. These symptoms would include breast pain when climbing the stairs or pain in the legs when walking uphill.

In some countries a doctor can make use of the fact that normal men have hard erections several times during a night's sleep. He can refer his patient to a sleep laboratory where the penis can be wired up during the night. If the penis becomes erect the normal number of times, it suggests that there is a psychological brake on his activities at other times. A novel device now marketed in the United States is a pocket-size erection recorder that is strapped onto the penis at home before bedtime with two straps that break when a certain swelling pressure is reached. With this device a man can find out how many times he gets an erection during the night and how hard it gets. This type of erection recording is not yet in routine use, however, partly because of the price of the equipment and partly because many men don't like putting their penis in a straight-jacket before retiring for the night.

On the other hand, since erection has two aspects (an increase in size and an increase in rigidity), in many cases of impotence an increase in size can occur but the organ may not be stiff enough to penetrate a vagina. For this reason, measuring instruments have been constructed to measure not only how much the penis swells, but also how stiff it gets. You can do this by adding weights to an erect penis to find out how much it can take before it begins to bend (the so-called buckling pressure). Scientists know that it takes about one to two pounds of pressure to open the average vagina and they can therefore predict whether an erection is good enough by its response to the buckling test. Not surprisingly, a heavily lubricated vagina has less resistance and can accommodate less rigid penises, an important consideration for men.

ADDITIONAL TESTS

Certain drugs, when injected into the side of the penis into the spongy cylinders, can cause them to swell and suck in blood from the arteries, producing an erection indistinguishable from the real thing and lasting at least twice as long. A single injection of such a drug in a man whose erection problem is due to psychological problems can give an impressive erection within minutes—and can bring a joyful tear to his eye. For such men, just the sight of an erection after a drug injection is the best therapy they could have wished for and often has lasting effects. For those who still need therapy, at least the drug has shown that the problem is clearly psychological and not physical. If it takes a long time for the drug to work or if the doctor has to double or even triple the dose before there are signs of life, it could indicate a blood-vessel problem.

A young man with circulatory problems due to damage or a congenital abnormality would be examined by a means of a special X-ray of the arteries to see where the blockage or damage is. If this is successful the referral would be to the surgeon or urologist for a bypass operation. For the older man whose major problem is that his arteries are clogged with cholesterol, surgery may be too risky, as may be the X-ray. But, as you will see later, other possible treatments exist.

If a drug injection causes a good erection but the erection shrinks quickly, a leakage problem may be indicated, and more sophisticated tests and referrals to other specialists may be required. A radiologist may be suggested to carry out a very special type of test. By sticking a needle into the spongy tissue of the penis and pumping in salt water, the radiologist can make the penis erect. By calculating how much and how fast he has to pump in the salt water after a drug injection, he can calculate whether the penis has sprung a leak, and if so how serious a leak. If he then injects a radiopaque liquid through the same needle and follows it using X-ray, he can actually locate the site of the leak. With a normal erection, the opaque medium should stay trapped in the penis. Armed with this knowledge, the surgeon can tie knots in the veins responsible to try to reduce the leak. Today this treatment can be successful in up to 60 percent of cases where leakage is the problem; the closer you tie the knots to the spongy tissue the better the result.

When there is the possibility that the patient's ills are caused by too little male hormone, it is possible to put him on a course of hormone tablets just to see what happens.

If the patient is a diabetic, there's a good chance that his impotence is caused by nerve damage. The same can occur in men with prolapsed disks and in men with a long list of special types of neurological diseases. In such cases, it can be helpful if the doctor gets advice from a neurologist. However, apart from the prolapse there is little anybody can do to rewire the appropriate electrical circuits, and this type of patient (along with the other men who are unsuitable for blood vessel surgery) are faced with quite different alternatives.

SELF-TREATMENT FOR IMPOTENCE

NEW USES FOR A RUBBER BAND

Around forty years ago, a resourceful, elderly man with an impotence problem and presumably desperate from the lack of treatment possibilities available at the time devised a simple apparatus consisting of a cylinder with a rubber tube at one end. By placing the cylinder over the penis and sucking out the air through the rubber tube he was able to create sufficient vacuum to cause blood to erect his penis. A tight elastic band over the base kept the blood trapped in his organ long enough for him to have intercourse. It is said that he used this technique satisfactorily twice a week for the next twenty years. Similar vacuum devices, with more convenient ways of pumping out air, are now in widespread use all over the world. Over 90 percent of men using these devices can achieve penetration and over 80 percent are satisfied with the results. The diameter of the penis has also been shown to be bigger than normal using the vacuum method and it only takes about two and a half minutes to get it pumped up to a working size.

Of course there are certain drawbacks. The elastic bands can't be left on for more than thirty minutes or the organ will probably drop off! Sometimes bruising can occur on rare occasions due to a small blood vessel under the skin bursting, which has little consequence aside from making the penis look like it has gone a round with Mike Tyson. And of course it can be difficult to ejaculate with a rubber band in place, although research articles assure that this is not painful and that it is simply delayed until the rubber band is removed. The use of constricting rings around the penis to maintain a sagging erection is not a new idea. In China, a ring made of jade, sometimes of ivory, was fitted around the base of the penis and held by a silk band that went between the legs and around the waist. Today, plastic erection rings can often be bought through mail-order firms.

TABLETS AND CREAMS

Yohimbine, a chemical extracted from the bark of a West African tree, is one of oldest aphrodisiacs known to man, and one of the few whose effects on potency has been scientifically confirmed and explained. It "fools" the spongy tissue of the penis into expanding and filling with blood. About 20 percent of those taking tablets regularly report an improvement in their erection, although only those men with a healthy cardiovascular system should use the drug because of its side effects on blood pressure. Another novel medicine that may find a place in the treatment of impotence is nitroglycerin, the same stuff used in the treatment and prevention of angina. This medicine is known to expand small blood vessels and increase blood flow. At least two research groups have shown that if a nitroglycerin gel is rubbed onto the penis before sexual activity, a stiffer erection is produced. The only side effect is that the partner can develop headaches during sex because the nitroglycerin can enter her blood through the vaginal wall and disturb the blood flow in her brain.

DRUG INJECTIONS

The use of drug injections to lead the doctor to the cause of the erection is one thing, but these same drugs are now also being used as a form of treatment. With the right dose, an erection comes within a few minutes and can last several hours regardless of how many ejaculations the man has. In some cases, the effect can be delayed, especially if the patient is stressed during the injection. Many a man having touched the depths of despair after a negative result with one of these drugs in the doctor's office has called from a pay phone on the way home to announce the joyful news that he is now the proud owner of an erection (probably much to the disgust of anyone waiting to use the telephone!). Those who are up to it can inject the stuff themselves in the privacy of their own home, and there are tens of thousands doing this in America alone. Such medication, however, is open to misuse, and if this type of treatment is not held under strict control the number of unwanted side effects will undoubtedly increase. The most important is priapism (from the Roman god Priapus) or persistent erection. In fact, with the wrong dose an erection can last two to twenty hours, which can cause permanent damage to the spongy tissue of the penis. Six hours has now been set as the limit before the man has to think about contacting a doctor. The treatment sounds barbarically simple but it is not dangerous and it works. The doctor sticks a needle into the sponge tissue, sucks out a syringe full of blood, and injects adrenaline, which then collapses the blood spaces and makes the erection disappear. Another problem is that if the injections are not done carefully and systematically, small painless lumps of fibrous tissue can develop at the injection site. Too much of this tissue can deform the penis, which can make sex painful, unless a partner is found with a vagina that curves in the appropriate direction. To reduce this problem American doctors are now restricting use of the drug to two injections a week, presumably with an extra thrown in on birthdays!

PROSTHETIC DEVICES

According to the experts, it seems likely that the first artificial prosthesis used for making the penis stiff enough for intercourse consisted of a rod or reed pushed into the urethra. God knows the experimenter must have been desperate! Not until 1936 did anyone get around to restoring an erection by surgically inserting something stiff into the spongy tissue of the penis. A piece of rib cartilage was chosen for this historic first operation, but not long after other surgeons began to implant pieces of bone. The problem was that bone was too hard to shape and soon began to be absorbed by the body, causing the penis to deform. Around 1947, an American named Goodwin, working with a dentist, constructed an acrylic plate, which he implanted into the penis on its upper side, and that solved the problem of deformation. The logical next step in 1960 was two acrylic rods placed in the center of each of the two sponge barrels. At first they were implanted the full length of the penis, producing a permanent erection that always pointed to the horizon, a situation that must have attracted admiring glances at the local swimming pool. Then somebody had the bright idea of making the rods shorter so that the penis was hinged at the base. This still caused the mass migration of elderly women from swimming pools. Gradually, flexible rods of silicon replaced the stiffer variety, and later models had the incredible property of being soft when they hung down and stiff when curved upwards.

And the best was yet to come! In the 1970s the first inflatable penis prosthesis became available. By squeezing a pump in the scrotum, salt water could be squeezed from a reservoir into hollow rods in the penis, causing them to expand. When the erection was no longer required, pressure on a valve caused the flow to reverse and direct the fluid back into the reservoir, as close to nature's own hydraulic system as you could get! Today, everything, including the fluid reservoir, is built into the penis rods, and expansion can be brought about by pressing a valve at one end and deflation by pressing a second valve at the other.

We are entering a new era in which impotence may not be the calamity it once was, an era when the ability to have an erection becomes a basic human right regardless of age, an era when so many treatment possibilities are available that the vast majority can be helped. It is a time when men can go with drug-induced erections for hours or that can appear at the press of a button and don't disappear after an ejaculation. Maybe it's now time to ask their wives if this is what they want!

13 MALE MENOPAUSE: WHEN THE LION LOSES ITS MANE

When a man gets old his balls grow cold.

The man who wrote this poignant statement on a restroom wall appears to have come to terms with what for many is the cruelest reminder of old age—the final and humiliating stab in the back for a once-proud male.

The sages say it can creep on us as early as our midforties, so imperceptibly, so insidiously that those who are smitten may be totally unaware that another of life's chapters is unfolding. But their friends, their wives, and their colleagues may notice subtle changes in mood and not so subtle changes in behavior.

> **The wife of a middle-aged man, upon seeing her husband flirting with a girl young enough to be his daughter, turns to her horrified friend and with a calm and knowing look whispers, "It's all right, dear, I think George is going through the menopause."**

Mirrors warn a man of the tell-tale signs and become mortal enemies. The peacock's plumes become faded, the lion's mane becomes moth-eaten, and the raptor's proud chest becomes a not-so-proud stomach. Finally, the sex organs, which in another time stood to attention for hours with a kiss or a fondled embrace, now stay hidden from sight, resistant even to the most extreme forms of erotic bribery. Some say it's all in his mind, others that he is simply reacting like a slave to preprogramed changes in his body chemistry. Some say it's old age, others that it is because the sex glands have staged their own unofficial strike in demands for an early pension. It's a question that has occupied the minds of research workers and psychologists for the last forty years: Is there a male menopause?

THE MIDLIFE CRISIS

One of the most conspicuous features of modern middle age is the onset of an adolescent-type identity crisis at about the age of forty-five, around the time when male menopause is supposed to start. Unlike male menopause, however, the midlife crisis is probably not precipitated by a revolution in the testicles, but by a revolution in the brain. This is an important aspect of maleness that needs to be understood if a man is to earn any sympathy from a bewildered and often frustrated partner. At this time in a man's life, the need to experience unenacted fantasies "now or never" happens—often at the same time he has the time and money to do something about it.

Unfortunately, this final fling before the gates close can cause havoc for the family and fill the last half of a man's life with bitterness. In its extreme form, a midlife crisis often involves dramatic changes in life-style. The French painter Paul Gauguin, who gave up his safe career as a stockbroker and went to the South Seas where he did his best paintings, has become the classical example for many discontented middle-aged men. It may involve changing a spouse, or the frenzied pursuit of young women as a reassurance against waning potency, or a change of jobs. He may astonish his friends by suddenly becoming interested in sports, buying a fashionable training suit, and training for the local marathon. After a whole lifetime of sitting on a sofa, watching television and eating junk food, he may start taking jazz ballet or decide that cycling to work is not such a bad idea after all. His reasons may vary from a sudden awareness that it is not only the neighbor who suffers heart attacks to the resignation that his middle-age spread will not disappear by simply ignoring it. The problem is that this frantic desire to turn back the clock can come all too late. A cardiologist's nightmare is the overweight, unfit, middle-aged man who suddenly decides to join the jogging brigade and do a four-minute mile in the first week.

The famous psychologist Dr. Charlotte Buhler concluded that in middle age and beyond, the most critical factor in adjustment was the person's self-assessment as to whether he or she had fulfilled their promise, rather than any feeling of insecurity or physical decline. Interestingly, men apparently see a close relationship between their lifeline and what they have achieved in their careers. If there is a chasm between hopes and actual achievements, a man may be very aware of his age and the fewer chances he has to fulfill his dreams.

THE DIFFERENCE BETWEEN MALE AND FEMALE MENOPAUSE

We associate menopause with the female sex and all the psychological and physical changes it may precipitate—depression, night sweating, weight changes, profound alterations in body function such as the disappearance of menstruation and the loss of fertility—like petals suddenly falling from a once delicate and exquisite bloom. If these changes do occur in men, they do so in a more merciful and kinder way. Most men are spared the sudden upheaval in their lives that menopause can cause in women. In the case of the male bloom, it can take years for erect stems to wilt and for petals to gradually discolor before the plant finally goes to seed. Of course many men will deny that these changes take place or at least resist the thought until it is no longer possible to ignore the evidence.

A SLOWDOWN IN HORMONE PRODUCTION

Let us examine the scientific evidence for and against a male analogy to the female menopause. It should now be becoming clear that just as estrogens are the chemical key to femininity, testosterone is the sex hormone that switches all of a man's bodily organs, including his brain, into the masculine mode. For twenty to thirty years, the testicles obediently inject this potion into the blood, giving daily shots of maleness to sustain men during their masculine pursuits in their reproductive years. But the testicles are not autonomous little Napoleons who alone decide men's sexuality. No, that privilege has been given to the pituitary, the pea-sized gland at the base of our brain, and even this is merely a slave to the whims of the brain itself. Although diminutive in size, the pituitary is the conductor in the orchestra of our hormone-producing glands. In men, luteinizing hormone (LH) controls the hormone factories in the testicles and is constantly taking audits of how much its factories are producing each day. When the level of testosterone in the blood begins to fall, LH will act to speed up production. Another hormone, follicle stimulating hormone (called FSH for short), is also made by the pituitary and is responsible for making sure the productivity of the sperm factories in the testes do not fall behind schedule.

Most of the testosterone injected into the blood by the testes circulates by attaching itself to binding proteins, and is therefore unable to reach out to the muscles, hair, follicles, and genital organs through which the blood permeates. In short, it is prevented from doing its job. In fact, only 1 to 2 percent of the amount produced is allowed to filter from blood to masculinize these organs. Some of the male hormone undergoes a chameleonlike transformation in fat tissue into estrogen, the female sex hormone. This occurs in small quantities, however, and rarely causes the body to grow breasts, sing soprano, or take on other female characteristics. Around forty to fifty years of age, something begins to happen that eventually alters this delicate hormonal balance. For some as yet unknown reason, a mutinous testicle begins to ignore the chemical commands from the master pituitary gland and instead charts its own course on a gradual downward path, dragging the male hormone with it. In desperate attempts to restore order, the pituitary, nudged by the brain, sends pulses of LH to squash the revolt, but in most cases this is to no avail and the levels of this hormone soar to record heights as if in a rage of frustration. To make matters worse, at about age sixty, the amount of testosterone transformed into its female counterpart begins to increase and in such quantities that the male organs begin to feel its vibrations. One of its effects is to increase the amount of binding protein, that chemical flypaper, in the blood so that even fewer testosterone molecules are allowed to fly free. Another effect may be to increase the size of the male breasts. Indeed, several scientists have suggested that this partial feminization of men may also explain why the prostate gland (which we will hear more about later) starts to blossom again around middle age with all the plumbing problems that this can cause.

> Two elderly men are talking: "Say, do you remember during the war when they used to give us saltpeter in our coffee, to keep us from thinking about women?" "Yes, why?" "I think it's just starting to work on me."

The scientist who discovers why the ovaries may suddenly stop working and why the testicles may gradually grind to a halt in middle age is worthy of a letter from the Swedish Nobel Institute. Is there a self-destruct device hidden in our testicles that is activated when the optimal time to produce children is past, or does it simply mean that the testicle, like most other organs, grows old and loses function? After all, it's difficult to understand why nature should provide a senior citizen with sexual machinery oiled and ready to go, when his heart and lungs tell him to slow down! Some believe that the function of the testicles slows down because the circulatory system carrying its blood supply gets blocked with old age or becomes damaged. Others have a theory that our bodies begin to recognize our testicles as foreign and send squadrons of antibodies to attack and weaken them. However, several groups of menopause researchers have noted that if you excluded from their studies those men who were chronically ill, who had psychiatric problems, or who were taking drugs, it actually appeared that even in advanced age, the testicles continue to do their job almost as well as they did in their youth. Their point was that the testicles have an impressive ability to resist the ravages of old age, but that a strong will can be broken by damage, disease, drugs, or depression, and unfortunately few of our seniors are in a position where they can avoid meeting at least one of these situations.

HOW TO COPE WITH THE INEVITABLE

Let us assume that in the majority of men there is indeed a decrease in this elixir of maleness, testosterone, after forty years of age—so what? What are its consequences? Before answering the question, let us remind ourselves of the three qualities of being male: fertility, the ability to produce enough sperm to make his partner pregnant; potency, the ability to produce an erection and have sexual intercourse; and libido, the desire to have sex. It's important to understand that a man can be impotent but fertile and have a high libido. Alternatively, he can be potent, infertile but have no enthusiasm for sex . . . and almost any other combination. Testosterone is almost certainly necessary for all three, but the amounts needed to sustain one activity may be quite different from the others. It is generally agreed that the incidence of potency problems increases as we get older. However, as we have already discussed, it is also believed that for impotence and low libido to be explained by problems in the testosterone department, then its production has to be taken down all the way to first gear. Healthy old men who have problems with their sex lives, who are not impotent because of circulatory or nerve problems in their penis, and who do not abuse alcohol or take lots of medicines, have only very rarely such low levels of testosterone. In these men the answer probably lies in their gray matter rather in their glands. On the other hand, in some men there is indeed a sudden and drastic reduction in the production of testosterone, and these unfortunate individuals can go through a classical menopause with impotence, loss of sexual desire, reduced testicular size, reduced beard and body hair growth, and vague symptoms such as tiredness and hot flushes. It is these pseudo-castrates who will gain the most from treatment with the male hormone.

We may therefore be talking about three groups of men. We have those untouched by the ravages of old age, members of the Charlie Chaplin fan club whose sex lives and testosterone stand like firm pillars against the storms of senescence. We have those who gradually bend in the storm with declining sexual activity and sex hormone levels, but in whom the hormones do not decrease to the extent that they can explain the potency and libido problems. Finally, there are those who are blown over by the first gust, who, because of sickness or drugs, show a sudden testosterone withdrawal and go through a classical male menopause. Recent studies indicate that the latter group represents around 10 percent of elderly men.

Fertility is acknowledged to decline as men get older, although this is rarely dramatic. Stories abound about octagenarians such as Charlie Chaplin making their younger spouses pregnant, and even a ninety-four year old has been reported in the scientific literature to enjoy the delights of new-baked fatherhood. In one study, fifty-five-year-old men still produced more than 75 percent of the sperm numbers ejaculated by men twenty-five years of age. Indeed, it appears that men still constitute pregnancy risks even at advanced ages, and women should not be deceived by the gray hair and backs bowed by time.

Fertility is one thing and rather superfluous for a retiree. But what about sex? If we look at the way sexual function changes with age, let us examine the good news first. There are no reports of shrinkage of the erect sexual organ with age, and elderly men become much more adept at delaying their ejaculation than in their youth when eruptions could occur at the slightest provocation. This observation agrees with a study by an American group showing that the threshold at which a man perceives vibrations to the head of his penis increases generally with age until the twilight years when even a pneumatic drill may not awaken it from its slumber. The news of more doubtful significance is that the testicles become a little smaller and the angle at which the penis stands when fully erect falls as the years go by. The force of the ejaculation is also reduced as we get older.

Now for the bad news. It apparently takes longer for men to get an erection as they age, and once it reaches the horizontal, it takes very little distraction to send it scurrying for cover. Like the magician said, "Now you see it, now you don't." The orgasm, if it happens, may be less intense but in general sexual intimacy is just as pleasurable as when our senior citizen was breaking hearts in the good old days.

How much of the changes in sex life, which are acknowledged to decrease with advancing age, are due to the fall in testosterone and how much is a matter of psychology? We have already seen that impotence is generally a matter of hydraulics or nerve injury or a combination of the two. In 1982, a doctor at Yale University presented data on elderly couples going for counseling because of sexual problems. Almost 60 percent of the men who began with sexual problems or saw their problems noticeably get worse, did so at the same time their wives were going through menopause. Vaginal dryness and the fear of hurting, feelings of rejection, postmenopausal bleeding, and even anger and frustration were given as reasons for the men's reduced interest in sex and their potency problems.

Let us expand this notion a little further. Men in middle age often have to come face to face with realities other than those on the sexual plane: physical weakness, fear of illness, insecurity about their status at work, threats from eager and more youthful competitors, fear of getting old, forced retirement, or the sadness and despair of lost opportunities. These blows to his stability, his ego, and his social standing may strike into the very core of his male pride, cracking its foundations and reverberating into the sexual sphere. Indeed, it becomes more and more obvious that psychological attitudes, especially in the male, determine his libido more than any other factor. As a man gets older, he can become particularly vulnerable to their influence. What nature deals out to the male sex may be kindness compared to what they do to themselves.

It is interesting that Kinsey in his classical book *Sexual Behavior in the Human Male* reported that although many aspects of sexual activity decline with age in the male, one of the features showing the slowest decline was the frequency of sex outside of marriage. The reason was attributed to the stimulating effects of new female contacts, a further strong indication that psychological factors are important in maintaining sexual interest. Thus it is vital for the preservation of the sexual relationship that the man not only give moral and psychological support to his wife when she goes through menopause, but also share the responsibility of maintaining a degree of novelty in their intimate moments.

Is male menopause largely a myth invented by men as a feeble excuse for their declining reproductive performance? Or is it invented by women to remind men that there really are no differences between the sexes? Some men do experience what could be loosely called a menopause because of a dramatic fall in their sex hormones, but these are few. In most men there is a more gradual decline in these sex chemicals over many years, which may or may not be responsible for the acknowledged decline many experience in their sexual activity. Ill health, alcohol, medicines, and, even more important, psychological problems all have damaging effects on this delicate process. Today, psychiatric counseling, hormone treatment, and the use of new surgical techniques mean that men no longer have to sacrifice their sexuality to the rigors of old age. But a precondition for reaching out for this help is that both men and women should be aware of the effects of the aging process on their sexuality and, even more important, refuse to bow to the cultural impositions and attitudes that say sex is for the young and not for the old.

14

THE PROSTATE: MAN'S HIDDEN SEX ORGAN

Most men are brought up with the idea that it's only women who have internal sex organs. They hear about menstrual cramps, PMS, hysterectomies, and endomitriosis, and they know that thousands of women make regular visits to the doctor to get their sex organs examined just in case there is something wrong. It is understandable that many men come to believe that reproductive problems are exclusive to women, and they never contemplate any anatomical similarities with their own reproductive system . . . until, that is, something goes wrong with it.

THE PROSTATE GLAND: FRIEND AND FOE

Ask the man in the street what a prostate does and where it is and chances are you'll get some vague replies: "It's what old men have, isn't it?" "It's got something to do with urinating," or "You can get cancer of it, can't you?" For many, the prostate is cloaked in mystique—a shadowy structure in the no-man's-land of internal sex organs—and yet, few men today will not at some time in their lives be uncomfortably reminded of its existence. Although diminutive in size, when diseased it can cripple the strongest and most robust of the young and give the kiss of death to the old.

In health, the prostate is about the size of a chestnut. It is wrapped around the neck of the bladder like a rubber collar, an arrangement that can have unfortunate consequences for toilet rituals when the gland is disturbed. (See illustration on page 74.) It sits at a sexual crossroads, allowing traffic along the main motorway from the bladder to the outside world, but now and again diverting convoys of sexual fluids from its side-streets down the same highway during ejaculation. In the middle of the gland, and along this highway is the "pressure chamber," which, as mentioned previously, plays an important role in ejaculation and the generation of the orgasm.

During ejaculation, the prostate squirts a mixture of sexual chemicals along with the other glandular secretions into the pressure chamber. Three hundred years ago, de Graaf, for reasons known only to himself, described the prostate as a revolver with six cartridges that could fire six seminal bullets before reloading. The functions of many of its secretions are still unknown. One called spermine is responsible for the characteristic smell of semen; others liquefy the seminal clump after ejaculation, allowing the release of the spermatozoa; another is believed to be a natural antiseptic, killing potentially dangerous bacteria in the vagina; and others may act to stabilize the DNA in the sperm's head. The gland is totally dependent on testosterone for its growth and function. Remove the testicles and the chestnut shrinks to a peanut and what was once a cascade of secretion becomes a dried-up trickle. Inject the same individual with testosterone and the process reverses. But this may not be enough, and the list of hormones that add color to our prostatic flower grows longer every year.

FURY AND HELLFIRE: ACUTE PROSTATITIS

For bacteria no organ is sacred but for our average one-celled gourmet the prostate gland must seem a tasty morsel of delight, filled with sweet things and conveniently placed at the end of a relatively short tunnel from the outside. An acute attack of prostatitis is best read about rather than experienced. It is not just the fever and back pains, not only the feeling of being ill, but also the unearthly searing sensation that burns to the very core of a man's sexuality. Urination turns his organ into a miniature flame thrower, and ejaculation, if he can muster sufficient strength, becomes so painful that becoming a monk is no longer a life-style to be scorned. His doctor sympathetically tells him to bend over, inserts two gigantic fingers into the rectum, presses gently on the swollen gland, and in between the tortured screams informs professionally that the diagnosis is confirmed. In fact, a good doctor would avoid this part of the examination because of the danger of pressing bacteria into the bloodstream and provoking a serious blood poisoning. Today, an aggressive use of antibiotics can usually disperse the intruders, extinguish the flames, and miraculously cause all thoughts of celibacy to disappear. However, for an unfortunate few, the agony can recur in the form of chronic prostatitis, which destiny has decreed shall plague them for many years to come.

PERIODIC PERDITION: CHRONIC PROSTATITIS

One day it happens. It may begin as a vague burning sensation "down there," something so mild it wasn't worth mentioning to one's wife. Or it might be something more distinct—a slight throbbing in the scrotum worsened by tight jeans or underwear or a strange discomfort from deep in the recesses of the body. Then again he may first notice it after a trip to the toilet or after an ejaculation—pain or an ache in the waterworks. It's registered and soon forgotten. But the next day it's there again, the same dull throbbing, gradually increasing in intensity and occupying his day.

For the first time disturbing thoughts enter his head: cancer? Gradually the symptoms take over, darkening his sense of humor, governing his social and sexual life. He may suddenly and inexplicably have a good day, when the symptoms vanish and he is filled with joy, love of life, and love of all his fellow men. But they return with a vengeance and he retreats once again into the gloom, reappearing occasionally to shake a clenched fist at his celestial maker. For some, it may also be the first time in their lives that they have indisputable evidence that they are equipped with sex glands. In this case, it's usually not only the prostate gland that causes misery but also another sex gland sitting high up behind the bladder and between it and the rectum: the seminal vesicles. Like a pair of rabbit ears, it sits on the same circuit as the prostate and often shares its infections. When both of these glands are chronically inflamed the condition is called chronic prostatovesiculitis, CPV for short. These chronically swollen glands press on surrounding nerves on their way from the spinal cord down to the external sex organs and surrounding areas. The result is a form of short-circuiting. The pain or aching feels as if it comes from the testicles and other regions but in fact originates higher up. This is rather like angina, in which pain is felt along the left arm caused by the short-circuiting of nerves from the heart muscle. Many men are understandably skeptical when told that the aching felt in or behind their scrotum, in the inner sides of their thighs, or in their inguinal areas is due to problems with sex glands situated around their bladder. In certain cases, the infection does physically travel further on the reproductive circuit, along connecting tubes to the epididymis, the structure that sits alongside each testicle and is responsible for maturing the sperm before they embark on their journey to the egg. When this happens, pain or aching in the scrotum, especially if it's combined with swelling, is a sign of an epididymitis, which can have disastrous consequences for the host's fertility.

THE DOCTOR'S EXAM

Traditionally men go to a doctor only when they feel a life-threatening situation has developed in their taboo area. When they eventually make that first journey to the doctor's office, it's often after months, even years of nagging from concerned spouses. The first minutes at the doctor's office are always a tense time for the male patient. Once he has gotten over the ordeal of explaining to the slightly deaf receptionist and to an inquisition of elderly women in the waiting room that he has a pain in his testicles, there's the added painful excitement (if this is a clinic visit) of waiting to find out which doctor has been chosen to hear his tales of woe. Having the door opened by a voluptuous female doctor who looks young enough to be his daughter can make even the most intense eye-watering symptoms from the sex organs miraculously disappear, to be suddenly replaced by a headache, chest pains, or any other symptom above the belt. Nevertheless, it's not long before the doctor has our hero touching his toes.

Once again, a rubber-coated finger is inserted through the anal opening and the prostate gland is carefully and methodically squeezed. One of several reactions is possible, bringing our learned friend closer to a diagnosis. Although the response may not be so intense as with acute prostatitis, there still may be the irresistible desire to scream and murder the owner of the finger, a reaction that would suggest an exacerbation of a chronic prostatitis. Or there may be no reaction—the exam is uncomfortable but not unbearable. Anything in between the two extremes would suggest different grades of a chronic prostatitis. Rubber fingers continue their detective work, this time manipulating those already all-so-sensitive structures between his thighs. A squeeze here, a sadistic pinch there, an anguished cry here, a tortured scream there, may tell the inquisitor that the inflammation has spread down to the epididymis. Painless small cysts and vague lumps on these structures broadcast that the inflammation has once been there and left its calling card.

And this brings us to an important point—the seminal vesicles. They are hidden behind the bladder and can be felt only through the wall of the rectum by doctors blessed with the longest of digits. Because of this, it can be difficult for him or her to exclude these organs as the primary source of the discomfort. Today with the help of ultrasound and rectal probes that can reach areas not reachable by fingertips, the secrets so long held by these structures are laid bare and doctors at last can get photographic, indisputable evidence of prostate disease and inflammation of the seminal vesicles. Without ultrasound the physician must rely on a combination of intuition and a long finger. In many cases of vesiculitis where the doctor cannot find clear evidence for the cause of the "male complaint," he may in desperation resort to an antibiotic cure. Unfortunately, in the vast majority of cases the cure is not given long enough, or the wrong antibiotic may be prescribed. When the unfortunate patient returns with the same burning pelvic organs he may be faced with a shrug of the shoulders and a doctor running out of alternatives.

It is said that you can always recognize a man with CPV by the eyes, which bore deep into his head; the brow, which becomes chronically wrinkled; the walk, which is tentative; the way he sits down, carefully; and by the unemotional way he recounts his symptoms like some tape recording. This last is because this is often not the first doctor to hear the tale but only the latest of many. Many have gone through so many "last resort" antibiotic cures that they have lost track. He trudges wearily from one doctor to the next in a desperate quest to save his internal organs and his sexual sanity. It may even happen that someone somewhere dares to suggest that it's all in his imagination—if all those antibiotics had no effect and if the doctor cannot find concrete evidence of something wrong, what other alternative is there? One can easily come to believe that a bleak future is in the making; no job, no marriage, only hate, envy, and paranoia.

But back to ultrasound, a technique to give back self-respect. Men who have gone for years in that limbo between psychic and bodily hell now are coolly told, "No you're not mad, my dear fellow, you just have vesiculitis." Oh, what sweet words; for a brief moment he loves his sex glands; they save his sanity. But after the euphoria, in mists of fleeting rationality, he asks, "But why me, and is there a cure?"

PROSTATOVESICULITIS: CPV

What causes CPV? Short courses with antibiotics in many cases have little or no effect, and there is little point in examining the sex fluids for disease-causing bacteria, because with normal detective methods they are either invisible or simply not there. But the evidence that there is something wrong with the sex glands is undeniable. The patient who jumps 10 feet after rectal palpation is using body language to make the same point. The man who has been three times around the doctor circuit pleading for help is not doing it because he likes reading sports magazines in the waiting rooms.

We do have photographic proof, and in many cases, but not all, the presence of inflammation white cells in the sex fluids is a clear indication that the immune system is fighting an unseen enemy. Because of the difficulty in finding a culprit, the wise men and women of the medical profession were pressed to invent names such as prostatodynia (pain in the prostate), something the patient already knew, or autoimmune prostatitis (inflammation due to an attack by antibodies), or toxic prostatitis (inflammation caused by accumulation of poisonous secretory products). At least the patient had a convincing diagnosis he could use to impress his friends at the next cocktail party! But how could you explain that long antibiotic cures—between six and twelve weeks with special types of antibiotic—could in many cases remove all symptoms, often after years of hell? So it probably is a bacteria. The reason why antibiotics have to be given in buckets rather than teaspoons is that the glands do not drain themselves well and have a relatively poor blood supply. Without this line of communication it's difficult for the body to mobilize the heavy artillery necessary for an assault.

Having found a comfortable niche in an out-of-the-way corner of its hospitable host, our microbial friend has little need to make its presence known in the sex fluids. Thankfully, with ultrasound pictures, for the first time doctors can evaluate whether the antibiotic has been effective in removing the intruder; all the evidence indicates that both doctor and patient have to be endowed with a great deal of patience before this is accomplished. An exciting development in this area is the implantation of antibiotic directly in the gland by ultrasound-guided needles and the removal of pus from out-of-the-way places. This revolutionary technique will dry the eyes of many CPV victims in the future.

Where does this bacteria come from? Is it sexually transmitted? Has my wife been unfaithful? The *why me* question often begins to dominate the conversation once the question of curability has been answered. Doctors are uncertain and confused. Boys who never have had sex can suffer from it, indicating that the infection can come from the bloodstream—for example, from an infected tooth, tonsil, or sinus. On the other hand, a large number of men who have previously had a sexually transmitted disease can develop the condition after a number of years. Some men can remember experiencing a dramatic and acute episode with fever, chills, and back pain that, after an antibiotic cure, later became the chronic and recurring condition that we see with CPV. Others do not remember ever having such explosive symptoms, and their condition occurs more subtly. We have still much to learn.

Stress and cold often cause a recurrence of CPV symptoms or worsen an already painful condition. Sex gland detectives have also discovered that CPV men often have stressful occupations, often with a great deal of responsibility. Under these conditions, decision making may not always be based on rationality but is more likely to be steered by painful sex glands. Historians have noted that Napoleon's poor decision making at Waterloo may be explained by a particularly painful bout of hemorrhoids. Hanging Judge Jeffreys's enthusiastic use of the gallows in the Wild West was also believed to reflect his personal battle with painful hemorrhoids, which worsened during particularly long trials. One wonders to what extent CPV has also influenced major historical decisions of our time!

The way by which stress and cold influence the symptoms of CPV may be related to the sex glands' blood supply, which is quickly diminished under these conditions. When this happens, the pain-producing chemicals produced by the inflammation are spewed out in larger quantities. In fact, it is said that one of the definitions of utter bliss is a CPV sufferer soaking in a steaming hot bath, his ecstatic moans in direct proportion to the volume of blood pulsating through his anemic gland. Although there is little concrete evidence to show it, it is also said that coffee and alcohol can worsen the symptoms of a CPV, possibly through their effect on the blood supply.

Finally, one important aspect of CPV should be mentioned: there are young men going around with the condition without being aware of it. The symptoms are often so mild that they are ignored. Often it is discovered when they come to the doctor because they have infertility problems and here is the tragedy: chronic untreated CPV can result in sterility. The infection spreads insidiously down the sperm-carrying tubes from the sex glands to the epididymis. Here they cause a local inflammation that can permanently block the hair-thin tubes carrying sperm from the testicle to the outside, in a similar way that local infections in the Fallopian tubes in women can also close them and prevent the egg from passing into the uterus. When this happens on both sides the prognosis for both sexes is extremely poor. The answer is in prevention. What is needed is a simple test that can be used in screening programs to identify those men going around with CPV with few symptoms. Today this is one of the challenges for sex gland researchers.

Yes, men do have internal sex organs, and it's time they talked about them and began to look after them. Thanks to ultrasound and a new awareness of the condition it is becoming clear that we are dealing with what may prove to be a new folk illness, a source of misery to thousands, a misery that men all too often suffer in silence.

THE BURDEN OF OLD AGE: PROSTATIC HYPERTROPHY

Puberty is a time of prostate growth when testosterone oils and turns the sexual machinery for the first time. Once activated, the prostate gland serves its master well for almost forty years. But then something strange happens, a part of the gland that has remained dormant since birth begins to grow. It's not cancer, but rather a blossoming of new prostatic tissue. By age fifty-five, 60 percent of males have begun to show evidence of these changes in their glands. In its confined space, this new growth presses away the original gland until it becomes a shadowy remnant—a second skin on the surface of the organ. It pushes its way in all directions, lifting up the bladder, squeezing the urethra, and pressing into the wall of the rectum. When a urologist sticks his fingers into the rectum he can feel this expansion, which he measures in terms of fingerwidths—from two, which is normal, up to four or even five. By gently pressing the prostate gland he can appreciate its consistency and distinguish prostatic hypertrophy, which is smooth but firm, from the more feared prostatic cancer, which becomes hard and uneven on its surface—all this with two fingers!

The enlarging prostate begins to make its presence

known. The bladder, lifted up in this unusual position, is more difficult to empty completely. The urine left behind, called rest urine, becomes easily infected and for the first time in the patient's long life he may suffer the problems of cystitis. In fact, this may be the first symptom of his prostate problem and the reason for his visit to the doctor's office. Urination can also become a problem, sometimes an embarrassing one. Gone is the time when a visit to the toilet was simply a brief interruption in a busy day. Now mental effort is required to press the urine past a squeezed urethra, and this battle with the bladder can take a long time. Toilet visits become major events and occur with increasing frequency even in the middle of the night, often three or four times. When these night visits begin to increase something has to be done, not only because it makes the sufferer tired and ill humored, but also because it increases the risk of an accident such as a fractured hip, which can have disastrous consequences for someone old and infirm. Because of the pressure on the urethra, the urine stream when it finally makes its appearance comes out as a dribble instead of a jet. A doctor can simply observe the man urinating or use a special apparatus to measure this poor flow. Not only that, often it can continue some time after the zipper has been closed. This alone is sufficiently bothersome to justify treatment. What scares most men with these types of urination problems is the risk of developing urine retention, when there is full stop regardless of the pleas and mental gymnastics over the toilet bowl. It can be because he ignored the first signs of bladder filling and the weight of the full bladder on the enlarged prostrate makes it even harder to empty. It can happen after a sudden cold spell or after taking certain drugs such as antihistamines.

Whatever the cause, according to Murphy's Law, urine retention will usually happen in situations that make treatment more difficult, for example, on a transoceanic flight or in a little hut in the mountains. Only a visit to a hospital or from a physician can turn a potentially life-threatening situation associated with kidney failure into a time of ecstatic and welcome relief, by simply inserting a catheter into the bladder. In the case of transoceanic flights it is often a good idea to keep a catheter lying around just in case or have a temporary one put in just for the flight. Repeated bouts of urine retention can cause kidney damage often without the patient having a clue it has developed.

Why does the prostate suddenly begin to grow again in this way? Man's closest friend, the dog, is the only other species to suffer from prostatic hypertrophy. Not even our monkey cousins appear to have prostate trouble, so why us? This prostatic rebirth has been linked by researchers to previous sexual activity, to diet, and to many other aspects of our life-style, but there is not any real evidence for a consistently identifiable cause. A theory growing more popular is that it is coupled to alterations in our hormones—a kind of male menopause in which there is a subtle shift in the ratios of the different sex hormones. It is well known that around the time when prostatic hypertrophy develops, men produce relatively more of the female sex hormones, the estrogens. In fact, the latest evidence suggests that this may take place locally in the gland due to the activity of an estrogen-producing substance. Already there are trials with drugs that turn off the activity of this substance so that the local levels of the female sex hormones can be reduced.

TREATMENTS FOR PROSTATIC HYPERTROPHY

Today the treatment for hypertrophy is usually surgical, although in recent years there have been some interesting attempts to reduce the pressure from the prostate by implanting special springs in the urethra. Before bringing out the scalpel, the urologist needs to take a closer look at the offending organ through a device called a cystoscope, which is introduced into the urethra and then slid down into the bladder.

For the initiate, the first sight of a cystoscope can be overwhelming. A man who has always believed his penis to be normal in size is confronted with the possibility that it is much too small to accommodate such a monstrosity of stainless steel. Even the knowledge that the urethra possesses incredible elastic properties does little to dampen the irresistible temptation to pull up his trousers and make a dash for the nearest exit. On the other hand, as those who have "survived" a cystoscopy can testify, the procedure is relatively painless, thanks to a local anesthetic squeezed into the penis before the apparatus is used.

With the patient relaxed, the cystoscope slides effortlessly into the penis toward the bladder, giving the urologist a worm's-eye view of the most important parts of the male reproductive system. He can now measure how big the prostate is and decide how much it strangles the urethra. The next step is to remove the offending tissue and relieve the pressure on the urinary system. The usual way is to cut and burn away the center of the prostate, rather like removing the core from an apple. This operation is called transurethral resection, or TUR for short, and takes place usually under spinal anesthesia, which means the patient can be an interested spectator if he wishes. Another type of operation, which is more complicated and takes place under general anesthesia, involves going through the urethra, burrowing through the lower abdomen, and attacking the prostate gland from above. Through an opening made just above the bladder, the surgeon inserts a single finger and with a smooth flick of the wrist removes the prostate from within its tough skin, like removing the fruit from a tangerine and leaving its skin in place. Whether it be like coring an apple or like degorging a tangerine the results are the same: the bladder and urethra, now freed from the constriction, can return to a normal, albeit weakened, function. Although he may never be able to enter the urine Olympics our prostatic patient can at least now hold his head up high at the public convenience and pee with dignity!

THE MALE CURSE: PROSTATIC CANCER

Like some dormant evil awakening from decades of slumber, prostatic cancer raises its ugly head in the later years of life, often with a well-earned retirement and pension just around the corner. This is a disease on the offensive. Almost 100,000 new cases have been predicted for 1991 in the United States alone, with a mortality of around 30,000 deaths per year. This makes it one of the greatest cancer killers of men in the West today. Since the 1950s, the incidence of prostatic cancer has been increasing by over 2 percent every year. Somebody once said that if a man lives long enough his prostate gland will eventually cause his death. Fortunately, a beacon of light in this gloom is that advances are being made in its treatment. As with many other cancers the earlier it is discovered, the better the chance of living out a full life. In fact, not all types of prostatic cancer bite with the same deadly venom and in many cases the time between receiving the diagnosis and leaving this life is so long that some other organ like the heart has delivered the fatal blow.

Why does this gland in particular and not other sex glands turn traitor and wreak cancer havoc? Who gets prostatic cancer? If we ignore the interesting observation that women apparently have a vestigial prostate gland tucked away in their reproductive organs, one of the few things we can be certain about is that it's men who get it or, more correctly, men with testicles who get it. In fact one sure way of avoiding the curse is by nipping off the testicles in early middle age. In this way the male hormone is removed, causing the prostatic bloom to wither and fade, unable to sustain the metabolic demands of a cancerous growth. However, mass castration of middle-aged men has yet to be proposed as a prophylactic measure to curb the disease. A third fact of life is that, as with many other cancers, cancer of the prostate is a disease of old age. What makes it so special is the dramatic way it makes its debut in the general population. As if some unearthly finger had pressed an ethereal destruct button at a preordained time, at the age of sixty-two years three months and one day it begins to make its presence felt, heralding the start of a cancer epidemic systematically decimating the elderly.

What sets and activates this time bomb within so many men? The question echoes around the corridors of scientific truth, a question that, thankfully, is being asked, but regretfully is still far from being answered.

THE JAPANESE CONNECTION

Forty years ago the first of several studies to see whether prostatic cancer had a predilection for a particular land or creed came up with an interesting piece of information. Whereas the American Negro male could boast the highest incidence of this type of cancer in the world, Japanese men appeared strangely and blissfully unaware of its existence. But even more intriguing, those Japanese who had emigrated to America at the beginning of the century had already by the first generation adopted not only a new citizenship but a prostatic cancer risk approaching that of their new brothers. A similar dismal picture was painted for Polish immigrants. Surely this indicated that there was some aspect of American life or environment that sowed the seeds of destruction or at least nurtured this deadly growth. But certain information complicated the picture. Studies showed that when a father had had prostatic cancer, the son had a risk of developing the cancer two to three times higher than men whose fathers had avoided it. Is this evidence that the disease is passed through our chromosomes or that we simply have enjoyed the same environment as our fathers? More interesting, although the African

Negro stands a much smaller risk of getting prostatic cancer than his black American cousin, he nevertheless develops it more often than his African white counterpart. This indicates that although something in our environment may be the major culprit, certain individuals or races may possess a bit on their chromosomes that opens the door and lets the mystical substance do its dirty work.

What is this factor with which we pollute our bodies and turn them against us?

One group of candidates are the so-called heavy metals. One of these is cadmium, an ingredient of car exhausts, cigarette smoke, and the dust that swirls around certain factories. Cadmium is special in the way it can be concentrated in the prostate gland by hitching a ride on a transport system designed for another metal, zinc, which is important for reproduction. Men living in areas with high levels of cadmium in the soil stand a greater risk of developing prostatic cancer than men from other areas. And it's been known for many years that men working in foundries that spew out great clouds of this and other obnoxious metals also have an increased risk. But it may not be just cadmium. People living around more heavily industrialized areas have double the risk of getting prostatic cancer than men in other areas. But before we all begin entertaining thoughts of emigration to a Pacific island, let's remind ourselves that the Japanese have smoked, driven cars, worked in heavy industry, and breathed air heavily polluted with metals just like Western males for many years.

The risk of women developing cervical cancer is increased if they make their sexual debut at an early age and if they subsequently have many different sexual partners, an observation that may be explained by the transmission of a virus during sex. The virus seems to cause an inflammation in the delicate cells lining the cervix, which can in some individuals blossom into cancer. It is probable that scientists had the same thoughts in mind when they began to ask prostatic cancer patients questions about their previous sex lives. Interestingly, a larger number of men than would be expected from the normal population admitted to an early and varied sex life, more frequent contact with prostitutes, and an episode with venereal disease in their dim and distant past. These apparent patterns became strengthened when one researcher isolated what seemed to be viral particles from prostatic cancer tissue. There must have been many scientists with long faces when a research article appeared showing that celibate Catholic priests in the United States shared the same frequency of prostatic cancer as the more licentious public in general. The alternative explanation was just unthinkable. And let us not do an injustice to the Japanese by assuming that their sex lives are any less active than those of people in other parts of the world. Like the heavy metal story, sexual practices could not explain the differences between the different races, so it was back to the drawing board!

What is it that the Japanese are exposed to when they emigrate to America? When one thinks of America, among other things one thinks of fast food—hamburgers, French fries, Coca Cola, and big juicy steaks. When one thinks of Japan one thinks of vegetables, raw fish, and rice. And here lies a clue: When one asks prostatic cancer victims in America and in Japan about their life-long feeding habits, several surveys come to the same conclusion. Men with large amounts of animal fat in their diet have an increased risk of developing the cancer. Not only could you explain the large differences in cancer incidence between the different lands by the average consumption of animal fat, but also within America itself, with hamburger and fast food areas having the highest incidence of this form of cancer. Not only prostate cancer but the incidence of breast cancer followed the same pattern. In agreement with this, in one of the latest reports from Japan, it is clearly shown that those men following the typical Japanese diet of green vegetables with large quantities of spinach and seaweed had far less risk of developing the disease than the newer generation of westernized Japanese who traded this for a hamburger and a double portion of french fries. This westernization of habits is presumably responsible for the latest figures from Japan, which indicate that prostatic cancer is on an upswing. It may also explain why Popeye even at an advanced age shows no sign of developing prostatic disease.

A CARROT A DAY KEEPS CANCER AWAY?

An interesting spin-off from the questionnaire studies was that in at least three studies it appeared that American men who regularly ate carrots, with their high content of vitamin A, had a lower incidence of prostatic cancer than men who did not. A very recent study in Japan came to the same conclusion and praised the properties of vitamin A and green vegetables such as spinach in hindering the expression of the cancer. Vitamin A has been known for many years as a chemical that, for largely unknown reasons, protects the delicate cells lining the body's organs from cancer-causing agents. These studies only added support to these findings. Theoretically there may be many other substances in our diet that under normal conditions serve to protect us from a cancer invasion. Vitamins C and E are known to hinder injury to cells that can generally increase a cancer risk. The essential trace element selenium may also be important, since men living in areas with small quantities of selenium in the soil have been reported to have a higher risk of prostatic cancer, an observation confirmed in laboratory studies.

So if the consumption of animal fat is associated with greater risk of prostatic cancer, what is the link between this sex gland and the hamburger? One possible connection is through the sex hormones. After all, the growth and function of the prostate is steered primarily by these circulating chemical messengers, particularly the male hormone testosterone. We have already mentioned that eunuchs are immune to this particular form of cancer. No one, though, has yet shown a clear relationship between the quantity of male hormone in the blood and the tendency to develop prostatic cancer. But cancer often takes a long time to develop and it may be more relevant to ask what the level of the male hormone was twenty years previously. It is also interesting that prostatic cancer was recently reported in a thirty-eight-year-old bodybuilder who for a number of years had taken large quantities of anabolic steroids, the synthetic male hormone. This is interesting because prostatic cancer is seldom seen before forty years of age.

That our food habits influence the levels of certain hormones has been known for many years. One study in the 1970s showed that if an African Negro is fed a Western diet for some months, the amount of estrogen, the female sex hormone, in his body increases while his male hormone goes on a downward path. Prolactin, a curious type of growth hormone known to encourage tumor growth in a variety of tissues, also appeared to be increased. Putting an American Negro on a typical African vegetarian diet had the opposite effects. So our diet does have profound effects on our hormones, such as testosterone, estrogens, and prolactin—hormones that are known to direct and influence the activity of the prostate gland. Here finally was a link—and we can do something about it. Breast cancer appears to share many similarities with prostatic cancer: Both are hormone dependent, the gland is influenced by prolactin and estrogens, and the distribution follows closely the ingestion of animal fat. A common factor for both cancer forms is currently being discussed.

A curious observation made by several scientists was that alcoholics rarely developed prostatic cancer. Postmortems carried out on hundreds of suspected alcoholics showed that whereas several of their organs including their livers showed all the signs of disease and destruction, their prostates stood out like shining beacons of health and vitality. This was despite the fact that their diet, with its deficiency in vitamins and trace metals, would theoretically have encouraged a cancerous growth.

The answer lies once again with the hormones. One of the side effects of the liver damage associated with alcoholism is that it changes the body's sex hormones in a female direction; the male hormone declines while the female hormone makes its presence increasingly felt. Without its chemical fuel the normal cells of the prostate have a hard enough time fighting for survival, never mind the cancer cells with their high energy demands. The difference between the effects of castration and alcohol on the one hand and the Western diet on the other, which all serve to reduce the levels of male hormone in the blood, may be the degree to which the changes take place.

How do we avoid prostatic cancer? The rules are simple but in many cases difficult to follow. Emigrate to Japan before puberty? A possibility, but maybe it's a little more practical to become regulars at the local sushi bar. Become an alcoholic? Again a difficult question, this time of economics, at least in some countries. Refrain from sex? Probably easier to emigrate to Japan and become an alcoholic. Take an active interest in carrots and develop a phobia for animal fat? Undoubtedly the most sensible of all the preventative measures. As a bonus you also reduce the chance of a heart attack, developing high blood pressure, and developing bowel cancer. For those unable to follow these guidelines but who at the same time shudder at the thought of getting prostatic cancer, there is always the one sure way of avoiding the misery—what could be the kindest cut of all.

THE SYMPTOMS OF PROSTATIC CANCER

The first symptoms of prostatic cancer can be remarkably similar to the first symptoms of prostatic hypertrophy because the cancer also expands and occupies space. This depends on which part of the gland becomes affected first. The patient may come complaining of problems with urination or a cystitis—a dilemma for the urologist who must distinguish the cancer from the kinder hypertrophy. Feeling the prostate through the rectum is one way of getting more information because the cancer makes the prostate hard and nodular rather than soft and smooth. The test is so simple and effective that many urologists recommend that all men over age fifty-five go regularly to their doctors to get it done. The problem is that not all cancers are so strategically placed on the back of the gland that they can be felt by probing fingers.

Another way of detecting a cancer is by carrying out a simple blood test, but unfortunately this is often performed when it is too late. Cancer causes leakage of certain chemicals into the blood normally found only in the prostate gland. The problem is that if chemicals can leak out into the blood, so can cancer cells and that means trouble. The ultimate proof that a cancer has developed is when a small piece of tissue is removed and examined under the microscope. Here the chaos of the cancer can be easily distinguished from the normal cells. The major aim of the urologist is to catch the cancer before it spreads beyond the borders of the gland, because such spreading can greatly reduce not only the chances of a cure, but the life expectancy of the patient as well.

This cancer's next port of call after the prostate is bone, and because of special connections between the spinal cord and the prostate, it often becomes localized in the backbone and causes back pain. Such symptoms are a nightmare for the general practitioner, who sees hundreds of patients in the same age group with the same type of back pain without it having anything to do with prostate cancer.

The good news for men just given the diagnosis of prostatic cancer is that it is usually a slow-growing cancer and rarely needs aggressive treatment. Most treatments strive to remove the effects of testosterone, which stimulates its growth. Without it, the cancer cell, like a normal prostate cell, behaves like an engine without gas. Its activity declines and its growth is slowed to a snail's pace. Traditionally, one sure way of removing the testosterone influence was to castrate the patient, often in combination with the injection of female sex hormones. Today, other more moderate methods are used involving the use of drugs that switch off the function of the testicles or neutralize testosterone's effects.

Another treatment is to kill the cancer cells while they are in the prostate by sewing radioactive needles into the gland that send out death rays to all tissues in the area. There are thus possibilities for treating one of the most widespread cancers in modern society, offering many men the chance of continuing their lives until they succumb to some other unrelated cause of death.

The prostate gland is like an unexploded bomb with an exceptionally long fuse, a self-destruct mechanism activated when man's sexual activity begins to wane, an ironic stab in the back from an organ that, in times gone by, was a source of exquisite pleasure and procreation.

MALE SEXUAL

REPRODUCTION

15 THE "DISCOVERY" OF SPERM

It cannot have taken too long for even the most primitive brain to see the relationship between sex and pregnancy, and to understand that a "male seed" transmitted from man to woman was responsible for making the woman pregnant. This is clear from the development of techniques in early societies to prevent this "seed" from entering the female during intercourse. Men began to withdraw the penis before ejaculation (coitus interruptus), and primitive condoms and pessaries were increasingly used as contraceptives.

Where was the seed coming from? The Egyptians believed that, like blood, it had its own circulation in the body and that the testes were part of this circulation. The enterprising Greek and Roman philosophers later modified this idea in their own theories on conception. More than two thousand years ago, thanks mainly to the wise words of Aristotle and Hippocrates, the general belief was that different organs of the body gave off an essence or spiritual substance that entered the blood. Blood was then transformed into the male seed or male catamenia as it was called. During intercourse, this male seed combined with a female seed or female catamenia, which was believed to be menstrual blood, and from the mixing of the two the embryo was formed. The essences produced by the different parts of the body helped to create the corresponding organs in the developing baby. Interestingly, and for reasons known only to themselves, both Aristotle and Hippocrates did not believe that the testicles were involved in the process of forming the male seed. We had to wait five hundred years for Galen, a Roman physician, to suggest that if blood really did turn into semen, it was in the testicles where the transformation took place. In the Middle Ages, our old friend, the theologian Albertus Magnus, concluded:

> Generation among men is through intercourse in which there is a mixture of the powers of the two sexes, from the male sperm which acts as a mover and from the female sperm or rather the female clear fluid as which the menstrual blood is the material.

It is apparent that Magnus shared many of the beliefs of the Greek and Roman philosophers. However, he emphasized, like Galen, that the testicles were probably the site of production of the male seed. Why? Because he noticed that during intercourse, the testicles were pulled up closer to the body, the reason for which, he argued, was so the testicles could more easily pump the seed to the outside.

At last, like a breath of fresh air the seventeenth century arrived and with it a time of awakening, a time of discovery, and a revival of classical learning. A new empirical and independent approach began to emerge in scientific observation. A man who epitomized this new feeling for observation was de Graaf, the Dutch father of modern reproductive research. In this book *Tractatus de virorum organis generationie inservietibus* published in 1668, he described the structure and function of the human male genital organs, a remarkable achievement when you appreciate what little had been written before. He made many important original observations. He showed that the testicle was a tangled mass of small tubes and not the amorphous porridge-filled bag others had earlier believed. He reached this conclusion because, whereas others had studied bull and human testicles, he dissected mouse testicles where the tubular structures are larger and much more visible than in other species. To convince the learned scientists of the day of his observations, he sent a dormouse testicle preserved in alcohol to the Royal Society in England. The outer coat of the testicle had been removed to reveal the mass of small tubes beneath. De Graaf concluded that within these convoluted tubes the male seed was formed.

Up to this time the general belief was that blood was converted into semen or seed, probably in the testicles. By careful dissection, de Graaf showed that this was not the case. He injected a colored dye into the blood vessel entering the testicle, but no color appeared in the tubules. He observed that the tubules connected with each other to form an organized duct system that he could follow out of the testicle, into the epididymis, and finally to the penis. But we can also remember de Graaf for doing one other service to science. He wrote the following in a letter to the Royal Society:

> I would like to tell you briefly that a certain ingenious man named Leewenhoek has devised microscopes which surpass by far those which we have seen until now.

By writing this, he brought to the attention of the most learned society of the time a man who was to become one of the pioneers in reproductive biology.

Antoni van Leeuwenhoek was a simple draper who also made microscopes that were better than those anybody else could make and which enabled him to make one of the most important observations in reproductive research. Johan Ham, a medical student from Leyden, was examining human semen under his microscope and saw something that puzzled and excited him. The view was filled with swarms of small swimming animals. He rushed to Leeuwenhoek to tell him about his observations. Leeuwenhoek, using his superior microscopes, confirmed that there were indeed small creatures in human semen. Looking at semen immediately after ejaculation, he noted a multitude of animals moving with snakelike movements of their long tails. It is difficult to conceive of the excitement that must have greeted these original observations. Leeuwenhoek drew them, counted them, measured them, and calculated how long it took for them to die.

His observations formed the basis of a classical letter he sent to the Royal Society in 1677: *Animacula in Semine* (Little Animals in Semen). His original description of the spermatozoon was in Latin, a language he did not know. It is speculated that this was because of the delicate nature of the subject. A further illustration about the attitudes of the time to this type of research can be understood from the letter that Leeuwenhoek sent to the Royal Society accompanying his publication:

> What I investigate is only what, without sinfully defiling myself, remains as a residue after conjugal coitus. And if your lordship should consider that these observations may disgust or scandalize the learned, I earnestly beg your lordship to regard them as private and to publish or destroy them as your lordship thinks fit.

Leeuwenhoek believed that what he saw were little animals, rather like the protozoa he had observed in pond water, but the fact that they were in semen immediately prompted him to note that they were connected in some way with the testicles and were concerned with reproduction. He stated:

> I have no doubt but that you yourself will agree with me in stating that the testicles have been made for no other purpose than to furnish the little animals in them and to keep them till they are excreted.

When the observations were published, people eagerly reached for their microscopes to confirm them. Wild theories were constructed to explain their origin. Many believed they were parasitic worms, which started a frantic search for worms in other body fluids. When the idea became popular that these little animals were concerned in some way with conception, there followed reports of small human beings called homunculi being observed in the heads of these animals. One microscopist followed this by swearing he had seen small horses in horse sperm and small cockerels in cockerel sperm! But still the most ridiculous was yet to come.

A famous physiologist, William Harvey, reported that he could not find semen in the uterus of a bitch soon after it was mated. He concluded that if semen was concerned with fertilization, then it must do so by giving off a spiritual element, an emanation or gas, which then drifted into the uterus and affected the egg. It was still not generally believed that the small animals in semen were concerned with fertilization. Harvey's idea prompted the belief that women could become pregnant only if they were exposed to the emanations or gases from semen. Many a respectable woman finding herself pregnant could blame it on an accidentally open window or door and arouse sympathy for it without damaging her reputation. In fact, we had to wait another fifty to one hundred years for conclusive proof that the small animals in semen, sperm, or spermatozoa as they were now called, were the agents for conception.

16 THE TESTICLES: THE SPERM FACTORY

I f you look through a microscope into the spaghettilike tubes in the testicle, you see a world of cellular chaos, or so it seems at first glance, because a more careful examination reveals the different cells actually follow an orderly pattern. In this long sperm factory, the round cells, which eventually give rise to the finished sperm, surround the circumference of the tube. Through several transformations, these cells gradually work their way into the center of the tube, producing concentric rings of cells at the same stages of development. As we work our way along the tubes there are also repeatable waves of development. During this highly complicated transformation, round cells gradually turn into streamlined cells with long tails, 160 million every day. During this metamorphosis only one of the two copies of each chromosome usually present in the body's cells is included in each sperm cell. This makes room for the single copy of chromosomes provided by the egg during fertilization.

HOW SPERM IS FORMED

How are these orderly transformations brought about? The key is a nursing cell called the Sertoli cell. Through invisible bridges, this cell makes contact with the different germ cells and coordinates and controls the different stages of sperm development. One way it does this is by controlling the availability of energy the cells use, providing the "milk" for their sustenance. By themselves they cannot survive because nature has decided that, like apples on a tree, they should be dependent on the nurse cell for their growth.

The different nurse cells work as a team. They join "arms" with each other, forming a ring and creating two different environments, one below their "arms" and one above them. The composition of the liquid in these two pools is very different. The liquid in the center of the tube, above the "arms" of the nurse cells, bathes the later stages in the sperm's development and is unlike any other of the body fluids. Anything that destroys this delicate situation, by breaking the "arms" and causing leakage of the precious inner fluid, stops the waves of transformation and the whole sperm-production process stops. Radioactivity, drugs, and high temperature—in fact anything that harms the nurse cells—decimates this nursery of germ cells. Recent research indicates that outside the tubes, the islands of hormone-producing cells, the Leydig cells, also have their activities tuned in to the different stages of sperm production, because testosterone is an important elixir for the nurse cell and her infants. When more testosterone is required, chemical messengers are sent from the nurse cell to turn up hormone production. At other segments along the sperm tube, testosterone production is turned down. In this way, the waves of production in the sperm factories are controlled, synchronized, and encouraged with maximum efficiency.

In the male fetus, the cells destined to give rise to sperm migrate from a place around the kidney down to the scrotal site where the foundations for the future sperm factory are being laid. Here they go into hibernation, waiting for puberty when testosterone and something called follicle-stimulating hormone (FSH) from the pituitary gland at the base of the brain can breathe life into them and switch on the production lines.

FSH does this by activating the nurse cells and getting them to create the unique chemical environment found inside the tube. From then on, FSH becomes the factory supervisor nudging the nurse cells into overtime when more sperm are needed. How does the pituitary know when production has to be increased? The answer is by a chemical messenger called inhibin, which is produced in the tube in direct proportion to the number of sperm that leave the production lines. With good productivity, large quantities are released into the blood and FSH production goes down. This causes the nurse cell to slow down and fewer sperm are produced as a result. If sperm production falls below a critical level, inhibin is produced in smaller quantities, FSH enters the blood again, and the nurse cell once again increases productivity. In this way, sperm production proceeds at the proper rate. If this delicate production line is irreversibly damaged or never gets started, inhibin is not produced and the pituitary pours large quantities of FSH into the blood in a desperate but futile attempt to stimulate the factory's activities.

When a doctor investigating an infertile man finds large quantities of FSH in the blood, it's a bad sign. It means that the sperm factories in the testes are damaged, which in the majority of cases cannot be corrected. In one type of infertility, called Sertoli cell only syndrome, the germ cells don't migrate down to the scrotum when they should. A glance inside the tubes reveals a forest of nurse cells devoid of vegetation, as in the aftermath of a forest fire with sentinels of scorched trees. In these patients, who naturally have no sperm in their ejaculates, the blood levels of FSH soar to dizzy heights in an attempt to spur production from its ghost factories. This and any other form of breakdown in the sperm factories can be easily discovered by removing a pea-sized piece of tissue from one of the testicles under local anesthesia, (called a testis biopsy) and looking at a section of it under the microscope. A malfunction at any one of the stages along the production line can then be easily seen by the accumulation of precursor cells before the block and the absence of other types of cells after the block.

Wafted by gentle waves caused by the contraction of special muscle cells in the wall of the tubes and carried in a stream of secretion created by the nurse cells, the sperm cells, now looking like the finished article, move passively along the tubes, out of the testicle into the epididymis. Special biological chemicals produced in certain segments of the epididymis make the proper adjustments so that the sperm can swim in a forward direction. Chemical scissors clip here and there, exposing molecules on the sperm's surface with which it can bind to the egg. In its journey down the tortuous corridors of this organ, which can take ten to fourteen days, many other invisible transformations take place. The DNA carrying the hard disks of genetic information is secured and made stable for the journey ahead. Finally, at the end of the tunnel in the tail of the epididymis, the sperm accumulate, awaiting ejaculation. (See illustration on page 74.)

WARM HEART, COLD TESTICLES?

When our ancestors looked down at their testicles, it's conceivable that once in a while they wondered about their function. But it would have demanded more of their intellect to ask why such sensitive structures should hang in such a vulnerable position between their legs. Why not out of harm's way with the rest of his organs—inside his body?

John Hunter, an English surgeon in the late eighteenth century, was probably one of the first to understand that the testicles were not just hanging there for decoration. He noted that men whose testicles had never made the journey down into the scrotum did not have children. The testicles of these what we now call cryptorchid men, which were trapped inside their bodies, were producing normal quantities of testosterone but something had switched off their sperm production.

It wasn't long before other keen observers began to understand that in normal men, the testicles were cooler than the rest of the body. In fact, depending on the species, this difference in temperature could be as much as 9°F. Men's testicles were relatively warmer but still 2°F to 4°F cooler than body temperature. Could this be the reason why cryptorchid testicles did not produce sperm? Testes researchers set out to prove whether this was true—at first with animal experiments. The testicles of rams, rats, and guinea pigs were pushed up into their bellies, plunged into hot water, and wrapped in woolen bags to warm them up, and the effect was always the same: sperm production dropped after a delay of a few weeks.

But it wasn't until an American named MacLeod coaxed some healthy young men into a fever cabinet and turned up the temperature to 109.4°F for thirty minutes that the impact of heat on human fertility became apparent. That short period of exposure was enough to depress the number of sperm in the ejaculate for fifty days after a delay of three weeks. The sperm looked exactly the same and swam just like normal but their total number was reduced.

So our testicles do need to be cooler, but why? Back in our dim and distant past when our cold-blooded ancestors swam in primeval seas, the process of making sperm must have become so dependent on the cooler environment temperatures that for some reason, and despite millions of years of evolution, our testicles still can function only when they are cooler. Indeed, as man and the rest of the mammals adapted to his new environment on land and to a higher body temperature, the testicles had to escape from the heat by migrating down from a place within his belly close to the kidneys, to the coolness between his legs where they could function properly.

This strange migration of the testes takes place in every male fetus just before birth, a reminder of our cold-blooded ancestors and their struggle to escape their cooler environment. Of course, on such a complicated journey it's not surprising that from time to time a wandering testicle gets stuck. In such situations, they need the help of the surgeon's knife or his or her expertise with hormones to coax them into position.

It soon became apparent that the scrotal sacs were not just bags of skin designed to hold the testicles in a cooler environment. In fact, the testicles had evolved elaborate ways of keeping the sperm factory working at an optimal temperature.

Most men are aware of the mobility of their testicles—their uncanny ability to move up and down with an intelligence all of their own, depending on the local temperature. Many men have experienced that "sinking feeling" after a hot bath or sauna and marveled at their disappearing act during a dip in a cold sea. This yo-yoing ability of our testicles is largely thanks to a special muscle called the cremaster, which yanks them up closer to home when you are cold and also when you're stressed. For some reason you can persuade this muscle to work simply by stroking the inside of the upper thighs.

The scrotum is not just any old bag of skin either. Its skin is much thinner than normal skin and has less fat so that heat can be lost from the testicles very efficiently. Its sweat glands are also special and appear to be activated by temperature-sensing devices in the same skin. The scrotum also contains a net of fine muscle fibers whose job is to vary the area of skin available for heat loss. When it's cold and they are in full operation, the testicles can look like wrinkled prunes.

But one of the testicles' most sophisticated pieces of machinery, developed to keep them cool, is tucked further into the body and cannot be seen or felt. The blood vessels taking blood to and from the testicle are very different to those found in other parts of the body. They are highly coiled and wrapped around each other. Because of this arrangement, the cooler blood leaving the testicle helps to reduce the temperature of the warmer blood entering it. The greater the number of kinks and bends on these blood vessels, the better the cooling effect.

Nature has clearly equipped us with means of keeping our testicles cooler than the rest of the body so that our production of sperm can continue uninterrupted. The major problem is that, as a result of his life-style, the modern male does not give these mechanisms a chance to work effectively enough. The difference in the temperature of our testicles when we are clothed or naked can be as much as 5.4°F., which is an indication of how effective our clothes are as insulators.

Several studies have shown that the testicles do not need much extra wrapping before sperm counts begin to suffer. Even when men walked around with a modified athletic support, which raised the testicle temperature by only 1.6°F., it was still enough to alter sperm count three weeks later. Small wonder that the current fashion for tight jeans and ultratight underpants all made of the newest and brightest synthetic materials pose a nightmare for gynecologists and andrologists who anticipate a multitude of calls for help when fashion eventually conflicts with the desire to have a family. To illustrate the point, several researchers have shown that men with sperm counts on the borderline of fertility can be rendered infertile simply if they wear tight underpants. An improvement in the sperm count was obtained if they were persuaded to wear the infinitely more practical boxer shorts. A more unpopular alternative, which also proved to be successful, was splashing their testicles with ice-cold water every morning before going to work! One can well understand the sentiments of the English andrologist who advocated that men go around wearing the Scottish national dress, the kilt, preferably without underpants. For those who wanted to avoid the kilt and the cold water there was always the ingenious piece of apparatus designed by Dr. Adrian Zorgniotti. The device contains a small pump that circulates cool water, or a water-and-alcohol mixture, through the cotton material of a testicle support. As the liquid evaporates, Zorgniotti claims, the temperature in the area drops by 3.6°F. Of twenty-six men who have worn the gadget because their testicles were too warm, ten have become fertile.

But men who wear tight underpants are not the only ones who can have fertility problems because of the heat.

Men who work close to blast furnaces or baking ovens are often knocking on the andrologist's door for help. And there are those, such as taxi and bus drivers, who sit on their testicles all day without ever giving them a chance to escape the heat. Regular sauna bathing is not recommended for men with lower-than-normal sperm counts; it could push them over to the infertile side. In one study, using a sauna bath eight times in two weeks for fifteen minutes at a time, decreased sperm count by 50 percent three weeks later and increased the number of badly formed sperm. At the present time, no studies have been carried out to decide whether men having regular hot baths suffer the same effects.

There are of course situations that adversely affect our fertility and over which we have no control. For many years, observers had noticed that many fever-producing diseases such as typhus, scarlet fever, chicken pox, and pneumonia could cause testicular damage in men but nobody knew the mechanisms involved, until relatively recently. Today the situation is improved by the use of aspirin, but several reports have indicated that a bout of fever during an attack of influenza can significantly decrease sperm count at a later date.

Another factor that we can do very little about is the climate, and at least one article indicates that if it gets too hot, then the testicle suffers. In Galveston, Texas, the pregnancy rate is inversely related to the temperature. In January the conception rate is 77 percent higher than in the much hotter month of August. Whether this effect also operates in other areas of the globe is not as yet known.

Cryptorchidism, as previously mentioned, is associated with infertility. But if the testicles are correctly positioned in the scrotal sacs at the earliest possible opportunity, then it is still possible to secure a good fertility. If there is a delay, then even if they are subsequently pulled down into their correct position they can fail to produce sperm, for reasons that will be discussed later.

Why is there a delay of three to four weeks between the

time the testicle is warmed and the time there is a fall in sperm count? In man, it takes a couple of months for a sperm cell to go through the different stages of its development and maturation. Although information is still scanty, it appears that only certain steps on this production line are temperature sensitive, the earliest stages being the most resistant. Once the testicle has been warmed, these stages are disrupted, but those preceding and following are intact. The result is a fault in the sperm assembly line that will eventually be seen when those that escaped the damage have been ejaculated. Scientists are still uncertain which cells are affected and which parts of their cellular machinery have been damaged, but everything points to the nurse cell, the Sertoli cell, as the one reacting to the raised temperature. When this is injured, its nursing function is disturbed and the most dependent cells succumb as a result.

17 INFERTILITY: WHEN THE SEED FAILS TO BEAR FRUIT

When a normal healthy couple decides to have a family, the fertility gods more often than not give their blessing. In fact, 65 percent will have achieved their goal within the first six months, 85 percent in the first year, and 90 percent after two years. In the remaining 10 to 15 percent the realization that something is wrong gradually begins to dominate their thinking and in some cases begins to govern their lives, their relationship, and their interaction with family and friends.

The inevitable question of blame raises its ugly head. Previously, women were thought to be the sole guardians of fertility. Today, though a man's pride in his sexual prowess makes it difficult for him to accept any responsibility, it's becoming more and more apparent that he may contribute to the problem in half the cases. Today 30 to 40 percent of male partners in an infertile union are under the fertile boundary. But only one man in a hundred who enters into a union wanting children will prove to be sterile and therefore be the clear cause of the problem.

To an increasing degree, barrenness in many cases is viewed as an interaction, a shared responsibility. In such a model, men and women can be given fertility scores, based on semen quality in the case of the man and hormone levels and the gynecological status in the case of the woman. A couple with two low scores have to try harder to achieve a pregnancy than those with higher total scores. One partner high up on the points scale could thus theoretically compensate at least to a degree for the other partner's low score. This helps to explain the large number of fathers with relatively poor semen quality and why new relationships can be barren when previous relationships on both sides have been fruitful.

WHAT TO EXPECT AT A FIRST CONSULTATION

Three hundred years ago, a man wondering about how fertile he was could satisfy his curiosity in the bathtub. The wise men of the day simply mixed the ejaculate with water; the quality stuff floated like oil while the second rate sank like a stone. Many countries had their own curious ways of determining whether men or women were sterile. One popular method in the rural areas of Eastern Europe, and a probable remnant of ancient Egyptian medicine, was to ask the couples to urinate in separate bowls onto a handful of barley or wheat seeds. Urine that caused the seeds to germinate within eight or nine days indicated fertility, no growth meant no babies.

Our forefathers also had rather quaint, simplistic ideas about the causes of male infertility. One popular notion in the seventeenth century was that semen should be the right temperature to fertilize the egg, and a variety of concoctions were prescribed by the apothecaries to warm it to the required temperature. Interestingly, a long penis was considered a disadvantage when families were being planned. Semen had longer to travel during ejaculation and was therefore too cold when it finally made its appearance.

Today, alas, the causes of male infertility are agreed to be frustratingly more complex, and the average semen laboratory contains in its inventory much more than a bowl of water. In fact, modern-day andrologists and gynecologists have access to a whole new generation of techniques and high technology that are revolutionizing our understanding of male infertility: exotic machines that fire laser beams at sperm and calculate how many are moving, how fast they move, and in what direction; computerized video machines that analyze their swimming pattern. Sperm can now be forced through a battery of tests to examine their endurance, to test their ability to penetrate mucus and eggs, to see how they react to certain motility-stimulating drugs. With critical eyes peering down futuristic microscopes and image analyzers, sperm detectives can now scrutinize sperm, colored with special dyes, for minute defects that may aid the doctor in forming a diagnosis. The pertinent question is whether this new technology really helps. Does it give hope to a despairing couple? Can it help men make more babies? To try to answer these questions let us take a closer look at what we learn from semen analysis.

If the woman has a normal menstruation and fulfills the normal gynecological criteria for getting pregnant, the next logical step is to send the man to a semen laboratory. The tests performed here are simple but also can save women from unnecessary discomfort and complex investigations if it can clearly be shown that the man is the cause of the problem. He may have no sperm at all or those he produces may be lifeless or incapable of movement. The sample is invariably provided at the semen laboratory, usually by masturbation. For many men this can be an unpleasant experience and fertility clinics are to be an increasing degree doing their best to provide special rooms where this can take place in a more relaxing and unstressed atmosphere. In some cases, this necessitates that wives also be present.

It should be obvious why the sample must be provided at the laboratory and not at home. It means that the analyses can begin within minutes of ejaculation which, as we will see later, can provide important information about the state of the sex glands. It can be guaranteed that it has not been exposed to extremes of temperature before the analysis begins, an important consideration. The sperm specialist can feel more certain about the ownership of the sample, and, last but not least, the samples can be provided under relatively controlled and standardized conditions. Having said this, there are relatively small differences between a sample taken after intercourse and after masturbation. In fact, after sexual intercourse, the sperm sample is actually diluted by the greater volume of sexual fluids produced under sexual stimulation.

THE FIRST STEP: EVALUATION
OF THE SEMEN

The volume of the ejaculate is the first thing that catches the investigator's eye, even though it doesn't tell anything about how many sperm are being produced. Why? As we have learned earlier, only 10 percent of the semen's volume comes from the sperm factories in the testicles. This is why men who are vasectomized do not usually notice a change in the amount of fluid they ejaculate.

Contrary to popular belief, the vagina is not the friendliest place for an inquisitive sperm. Its high acidity discourages the growth of bacteria and reduces the chance of infections spreading up to more important regions. Aside from providing a mobile swimming pool for the sperm, one of the functions of the seminal fluid is to reduce this acidity so that at least for the short time the sperm are present, it becomes a more hospitable place. Normally, the volume of semen ejaculated (about a teaspoonful) is sufficient to do this. If the volume is too small, the sperm's chance of surviving the acid bath are slim. How much fluid a man produces is dependent on the activities of his sex glands, but the amount appears to be surprisingly constant for the same individual when collected under the same conditions. The reasons for this are unknown. It may be related to hormones, to the size of the glands, or to their nerve supply.

Small semen volumes would thus reduce a fertility score even when the number of sperm produced is normal.

Another feature of the semen sample important in semen evaluation is its consistency immediately after and a short time after ejaculation. Normally, semen is jellylike at ejaculation. Then, within a short time at room temperature (even faster in the vagina), this seminal clump gradually melts thanks to the action of those special jelly-eating enzymes which arc made in the prostate gland. The possible reasons why nature has decided that sperm should be jellylike when the semen leaves the body have been discussed in an earlier chapter. Having reached its destination, the melting process allows the release of the sperm for their assault. Inflammation of the sex glands (for example, by bacteria) can alter the composition of their secretions and interfere with this delicate process of clumping and melting of the ejaculate and reduce the chances for a successful transport of sperm into the cervix. Too thick and the sperm cannot swim free, too thin and they may swim free too soon before they can react to the semen chemicals.

HOW IMPORTANT IS SPERM COUNT?

How many sperm a man produces is of course important. The greater the number of sperm entering the vagina, the greater the chance of fertilizing the egg. However, sperm count is not so decisive as first thought. The normal number of sperm produced per ejaculate is between 100 and 500 million (about 60 to 150 million per milliliter). Of this horde, only an elite 2,000 will reach the cervix, and of these, a mere 200 will reach the egg. A man producing too few sperm is called oligospermic (from the Greek *oligos*, meaning few).

But who decides what is too few? In fact, the recommended limit has decreased with the years. Twenty years ago a man who had 40 million sperm per milliliter was considered oligospermic. This has sunk to 20 million and in some countries to 10 million per milliliter. It appears that other characteristics of the sperm also appear to be more important. In fact, a surprising number of fathers consulting doctors for contraceptive advice would be considered oligospermic: 20 percent less than 20 million and 10 percent less than 11 million sperm per milliliter. Despite this, in the majority of cases men with low sperm counts are given low fertility scores.

Before visiting a semen laboratory, the man will be asked to abstain from sex or masturbation for at least three days. The reason is simple. The sperm stores of the human male are not equipped for frequent intercourse. In fact, two ejaculations within twelve hours can send the most fertile man plummeting into the land of the infertile, at least temporarily. In one study, medical students were asked to provide semen samples every eight hours by masturbation. Not unexpectedly, with the second sample, their sperm counts were already nothing to write home about, and subsequent samples dragged their fertility scores down even further into the murky depths of sterility. After a well-earned rest of three days their fertility potential had once again been restored. With this in mind, it is not surprising that the doctor consulted may probe a little into a patient's sex life.

Conversely, infrequent sex can also reduce a fertility score, not only because the man has less chance of depositing his sperm around ovulation time, but also because the longer the sperm are kept hanging around in the tail of the epididymis, the less vigorous they become. Fuel tanks run dry, bodies become corroded, and what were once sleek powerhouses of energy become ready for the scrapyard. If our man remains celibate for more than twelve days, these sperm begin to leak out in relatively large quantities into the urine, a natural way of relieving the pressure and making room for newly produced sperm.

SPERM QUALITY VS. SPERM QUANTITY

How many sperm are deposited in the vagina is one thing, but as pointed out earlier, this is not enough to set the investigator's mind at rest. He must now scrutinize those sperm he finds. How many are living? How do they move? What do they look like? Are they streamlined Ferraris or bumbling old Fords? Are they equipped to withstand the long journey ahead of them? After all, the woman accepts only the best. Inferior sperm may make damaged or inferior babies.

How does a woman ensure that it is a healthy sperm that finally penetrates the egg? She creates obstacles. Her cervical secretion becomes a myriad of tiny tunnels, a maze that only the fittest can overcome. The exhausted, the abnormal, and the slow-moving sperm get tangled up in its substance like careless flies in a spider's web. A large number of these misfits in a semen sample will reduce its fertility score, because the sperm researchers know that such sperm have little chance of passing through the cervical barrier. But nature can be tricked. Gynecologists can give even poor-quality sperm a better crack at the egg by depositing them on the other side of the barrier with artificial insemination. With in vitro fertilization, almost all of the natural barriers have been removed. Under these circumstances, it is only the coat that surrounds the egg that can sort the strong from the weak. So how a sperm looks is important. The stranger they look the greater the odds against them.

Twenty years ago doctors could discern and register only the most obvious abnormal features—too many heads, too many tails, swollen heads, pin heads. Today our instrumentation is more sophisticated and doctors can discern other more subtle attributes of the sperm cell that may not be quite right, and may be enough to stop it from penetrating the egg. Applying such criteria we see that even a normal healthy male of proven fertility can under normal conditions produce 40 to 50 percent abnormal sperm. Almost half of what the human factory produces seems to be destined for the scrap heap. Do these mutants serve a purpose? Do they in some way ensure the overall success of the mission, offering their lives like kamakazis? Some researchers emphasize that the appearance of such large numbers of less-than-perfect sperm simply indicates the delicacy and fragility of the process of making these cells, and its susceptibility to such environmental agents as radiation and chemicals. As we will see later, the list of these potentially damaging influences grows longer every year—from tight underpants to lead poisoning.

A man with a large number of abnormal-looking sperm is called teratozoospermic, from the Greek word *teratos,* meaning monster. Some men produce sperm that have the same fault on the production line—a head put on the wrong way or a kinky tail, for example. In these cases, when the fault is in all production models, a faulty chromosome is often the cause—maybe the man lacks a gene that directs the assembly of part of the steering mechanism or an engine component on the sperm production line. Thankfully, this genetic problem is not common, because there is little a specialist can do to make the situation better. The vast majority of teratozoospermic men produce sperm with different defects, almost as if the whole assembly line has gone berserk.

It is obvious that a structural defect will decide to a large extent whether sperm swim like dolphins or turtles, which brings us to another important characteristic of the sperm cell—its motility. Do they swim fast? Do they swim straight? It helps very little if a man produces millions of streamlined sperm if they don't have enough stamina to reach the egg or if their tail makes them go in circles. A new generation of tests and measuring devices can provide information on how many are swimming forward and their speed. In terms of speed and motility, we have certain reference values for what can be considered normal. A man who produces on several occasions a large number of slowly swimming sperm is called asthenozoospermic, which literally means sperm lacking in strength. Asthenozoospermia also appears to have many causes, from genetic to environmental.

An important point is that generally the greater the sperm output of the testicular factories, the better the quality of their product. The sperm are often more streamlined and swim faster. When the sperm count is lower it seems that something goes wrong with quality control. An oligospermic man has less chance of impregnating his wife than the next man not only because he has fewer sperm, but also because quite often those few he has are poor swimmers and don't look healthy. In fact, infertility more often than not is a combination of several problems. It is very rare that we see men with normal sperm counts and normal appearance but poor motility, or see men with normal sperm count and motility but abnormal-looking sperm.

Even though it may often be difficult for a doctor to put his finger on a specific reason for poor semen quality, in a large number of cases (almost 90 percent) he can get strong clues by talking to the patient and by carrying out a simple examination. There is available a whole library of information about factors that are known to interfere with male fertility and that may strengthen his suspicions—a previous illness, the patient's occupation, his life-style. The size and appearance of the testicles, the distribution of body hair, palpation of the prostate—all are important pieces in the puzzle. What are some of the more common reasons for male infertility?

CAUSES OF MALE INFERTILITY

LACK OF FREQUENCY IN INTERCOURSE

It may seem unnecessary to advise couples that if they want children they should have intercourse, but from time to time, fertility doctors have to do just that! For instance, some men married to extremely fat women have thought they have been having normal sex, but when their spouses have been checked by their gynecologists they were still virgins! In these cases, the men's penises had not gotten further than the body folds surrounding the real article.

In one American study, 5 percent of the cases of male infertility could be explained by the man's impotence. Everybody has different ideas of what constitutes a normal frequency of intercourse, but it is clear that those who regard once or twice a month as normal would be gambling on a pregnancy with the odds very much against them. At the same time an extremely high frequency of intercourse would never give the sperm stores a chance to recover, especially those who have low fertility scores. In 2 percent of the cases, the men have problems with their ejaculations. For some, the sperm never enter the vagina and because of retrograde ejaculation are sent the wrong way into the man's bladder. These men can often tell the doctor that the first urination after sex is always cloudy. In these cases, either the sperm have to be harvested from the urine after some chemical tricks and inseminated into the partner or the bladder neck has to be adjusted so that it can close during ejaculation.

> A party of astronauts on Venus ask to be shown how the Venusians have babies and are shown a complicated machine: A button is pushed, a tape is fed into the machine with the baby's required characteristics, the wheels whir, there is a slight blue explosion, and the Venusian baby comes out of a slot. "Now," says the Venusian leader, "how do you Earth people make babies?" After a hurried discussion, one of the female astronaut volunteers—for the sake of interplanetary relations—and the astronaut leader has intercourse with her on the table. "Very interesting," says the Venusian leader. "Now, where's the baby?" "Oh, the baby won't be born for nine months yet," says the astronaut. "Well then, what was the big hurry there at the end?"

HORMONAL IMBALANCE

Sperm factories need the right mixture of hormones to keep their production lines running. One of the most important hormones is testosterone. In the vast majority of cases, the hormones are in correct balance. But it has been calculated that approximately 10 percent of infertile men can blame their hormones for their problems. In some cases there is not enough luteinizing hormone, the hormone produced by the pituitary gland, and that controls the production of testosterone. In other cases, the production of male hormone is reduced due to abnormally high levels of another hormone produced by the pituitary, prolactin. The pieces of the puzzle fall into place when the specialist orders a battery of hormone tests. The good news is that in the majority of cases these hormonal problems can be corrected. Drugs, obesity, and stress can all reduce the levels of the male hormone and disturb the sperm production lines.

VARICOSE VEIN OF THE TESTICLE

The importance of keeping the testicles cool has been emphasized in an earlier chapter. In connection with this, it's appropriate to mention what may be one of the commonest causes of poor semen quality: the varicocele. The varicocele is a varicose vein of the testicle. It occurs on the left side more frequently than on the right and the larger versions are often described as feeling like "a bag of worms." Why it appears is still hotly debated. Perhaps it is an inherited weakness in the vein's wall (did the mother often have problems with varicose veins?) or there may be a disturbance in the reproductive anatomy causing too high a pressure in the system. Physicians are still not sure. The result is a damming up of blood on the same side, which may interfere with the cooling mechanisms of the testicle and cause an increase in the local temperature of 2 to 3 degrees. This temperature increase can be visualized by the fertility doctor using either heat-sensitive cameras or heat-sensitive paper. As mentioned earlier, the consequences of even a slight elevation in temperature can be a dramatic decline in semen quality; two thirds of men with varicoceles have a combination of teratozoospermia and asthenozoospermia. Thankfully, in many cases this abnormality can be corrected by a relatively minor operation in which the offending vein is simply "knotted" higher up, which often leads to an improvement in fertility score. Tens of thousands of such operations are carried out in the United States every year. The problem is that although as many as 39 percent of infertile men have a varicocele, the same is also true for 10 percent of fertile men, indicating that in many cases it may not be the primary cause of the fertility problem.

LIFE-STYLE

It is difficult to gauge the impact of a person's life-style on his fertility score. Clearly, in some cases excessive indulgence may contribute to reduced semen quality. Smoking is controversial and researchers argue about its significance. The majority of studies have failed to reveal a significant relationship between the number of cigarettes smoked and sperm quality. In contrast, evidence for the negative effects of alcohol are well documented. Alcohol can affect fertility in a number of ways: it has direct effects on sperm, which understandably swim erratically when under the influence; it reduces the secretion of the male hormone and causes sperm production to close down; and it reduces potency. How much alcohol is necessary to set these changes in motion is still unknown.

DRUGS AND MEDICINES

The process of making a sperm is a delicate one. Certain steps are extremely sensitive and the least deviation from normal is enough to cause a problem. Certain drugs are notorious for the way they can shut down sperm production. Among them are cancer-killing medicines, certain antibiotics in high doses, and certain nerve medicines. These are extreme examples, but what of the more common medicines: pain-killers, heart medicines, asthma drugs, other antibiotics? The list grows longer every year, but little is known about their effects on the testes or the way they may interact with each other. Thankfully, pharmaceutical companies now are responsible for the side effects their products may cause, which hopefully will increase the flow of information to the doctor about potential effects on fertility. It is clear that identifying medicine use is an important aspect of the doctor-patient interview.

ENVIRONMENTAL POISONS

The potential adverse effects of environmental factors on male and female fertility is currently attracting great interest from several grant-giving institutions in this country, in some cases spurred on by the belief that the general semen quality of the population has declined over the last twenty years. Certain occupations expose men to chemicals that at high concentrations are known to disturb sperm production. Heavy metals—lead in particular—are notorious for such effects. Several studies of men working in battery factories have shown a direct relationship between the levels of lead in their blood and reduced fertility scores. In one case, 93 percent of those exposed to the highest concentrations of lead had fertility problems. Welders also apparently breathe in large quantities of metal particles, which may affect their semen quality. In a German study, welders were more frequent visitors to an infertility clinic than many other occupations. Danish scientists have shown that those welding stainless steel had the poorest semen quality. "Organic solvents" is a term that also sends shivers down the fertility investigator's spine. Exposure to several different types in the chemical industry—toluene, carbon disulphide (paper industry), ethylene glycol—have been shown to depress semen quality. Several case reports are published of painters whose fertility score increased when they changed jobs.

But what about the man in the street—the man who walks to work every morning amid clouds of pollution spewed out by passing automobiles? What about the man who eats food with all those strange-sounding chemical additives that we are told are harmless, or the man who washes his plates in chemical detergents without rinsing them? What of the clean-living man who drenches himself in aftershave and spends the rest of the day breathing it in or the one squirting fluorocarbons under his armpits? Can these activities push those men with already borderline fertility scores into sterility?

ANTIBODIES FROM THE IMMUNE SYSTEM

Sperm are regarded as foreign by our immune systems because they are unlike any other cell in the body. To keep the immune system from attacking the sperm, nature has surrounded the sperm factories with special walls that keep out the immune system's killer cells. Women's bodies also have a variety of methods to prevent a man's sperm from being discovered by her immune system as it travels toward her cervix. Unfortunately, from time to time, the system fails and both the woman and man begin to produce antibodies to the surface of sperm, with disastrous consequences for fertility. Clothed with these antibodies before ejaculation (if the man is responsible) or on the way to the egg (if the woman is responsible) the affected sperm cells find it harder to swim, harder to become unclumped, and harder to penetrate the egg. Suspicions are soon raised when inspection of the semen sample shows sperm massed together in clumps like the snakes on Medusa's head.

Why does this happen? Presumably at some time the defenses protecting the sperm from the immune system have broken down. Vasectomized men often produce large quantities of these antibodies partly because sperm can leak out at the operation site and be exposed to the immune cells. When this happens it can reduce their chances of becoming fertile again, even after the tubes from the testicles are rejoined. A previous infection in the male reproductive tract has also been considered a possible factor, as prostatitis or an epididymitis may break down the walls protecting the sperm from the immune system. The number of men with this problem is relatively low—approximately 1 to 3 percent of those attending a fertility clinic. However, it may be that many sneak through this first screening simply because the quantity of antibodies is not sufficient to cause clumping of the sperm. In these cases, there may be sufficient amounts of antibodies stuck to the heads or tails of the sperm to interfere with egg penetration or to slow them down sufficiently to stop them getting to the right place at the right time. Today, there are sensitive blood tests that can identify this problem. The affected men can then be given a special type of hormone treatment for two to three months. This can temporarily dampen the immune cells' activity, reduce the quantities of antibodies, and clean up the sperm sufficiently to increase the chances of a pregnancy.

INFECTION WITHIN THE REPRODUCTIVE SYSTEM

When scrutinizing semen samples, the sperm investigator from time to time notices that the sperm under the microscope are not alone. Often they are mixed with white blood cells, tell-tale signs that there may be a infection lurking somewhere in one or more of the internal sex organs. In many cases, the sperm in the same ejaculate are of poorer quality, indicating that the infection has caused damage. Often the producer of the semen sample has not had any pain or discomfort from the region, and, even stranger, the culture of the semen sample rarely reveals the presence of the offending bacteria. And here lies the tragedy. Because there are no symptoms, our aspiring father may have gone years with his unwelcome guests, insidiously weaving webs of destruction throughout his sex glands.

Chronic and acute inflammation are known to disturb glandular function, which may lead to undesirable changes in the composition and consistency of the semen soup, and may, in a way that is not clearly understood, alter how many sperm appear in the ejaculate and the way they look and move. Even more alarming is the report that bacteria have been seen attached to the sperm, which means they can continue their waves of destruction inside the woman and, at the very least, infect the egg after fertilization. Many a gynecologist has achieved a pregnancy by treating the man with antibiotics, which may have to be taken for several months. Often this has been a last resort even when white blood cells have not been seen in the semen sample. These quiet infections can be frustrating to the specialist, who may have to rely on a sixth sense.

Approximately 20 percent of men coming to the fertility clinic have earlier had a child with the same partner but now have difficulties with a second. Under these conditions, a quiet infection coming on after the conception of the first child is the logical explanation. Of course, bacteria and viruses can also attack the sperm production lines directly, but cases of testicular infection are seldom silent and are easily remembered by the patient. Mumps is probably the most notorious, and in 25 percent of the cases the virus attacks the testicles. Happily, in about 70 percent of the cases the damage is only on one side, leaving the other factory to expand and take over production.

BLOCKAGES IN THE EPIDIDYMIS

As explained earlier, when the size of the testicles is normal it indicates that the sperm factories are in full swing. Testicles less than about 1½ inches at their greatest diameter indicate problems with sperm production, which generally decreases in proportion to the testicle's volume. If the semen sample is at the same time empty of sperm, it suggests that somewhere there is a block, and since there are two sperm factories there have to be two obstructions.

In 2 percent of men attending an American infertility clinic, the cause of this blockage was that the tubes from the testicles to the outside had failed to develop in the developing embryo. Since this flaw is also associated with defects in certain of the sex glands, these men often have small semen volumes. In other cases, these blockages are caused by bacteria or possibly viruses, with Chlamydia as a possible Public Enemy Number One. When you stop to consider how hair thin the tubes in the epididymis are, it is understandable that a local infection followed by the deposit of connective tissue fibers can easily lead to blockage of important canals. It has been calculated that in 4 to 8 percent of infertility cases (depending on the study), this type of blockage can explain the poor semen quality, more often than not in the epididymis. An English report ten years ago showed that over 20 percent of men routinely autopsied at a large hospital had complete obstructions in one or both of their epididymides. Can men with such a blockage be treated? Dexterous surgeons have managed to make bypasses around blocks in the epididymis. However, it seems to be vital that the blocks are not too close to the testicle. There are no shortcuts to the process of sperm "ripening," which takes place in the long tubes of the epididymis; if a sperm makes it through the bypass too soon, it is often a poor swimmer and will be unable to penetrate the egg.

SPERM THAT ARE INCAPABLE OF PROPULSION

Now and again, the sperm specialist may look through his microscope and witness a graveyard of sperm cells, all looking normal but apparently stone dead. Special dyes can often show that they are alive but simply incapable of propulsion. In these men, because of a fault in their chromosomes, the sperm lack an important part of their transmission, like having a car with a broken clutch. The sperm tail lies impotent and is incapable of generating the whiplash movement necessary to propel it forward. In some cases, this fault affects all the cells in the body with cilia, which are after all only shortened versions of a sperm tail. In the case of afflicted ciliated cells that line the air tubes in the lungs, instead of wafting mucus-carrying bacteria up and out of the lungs, they allow it to stagnate and cause infection. This is why the fertility investigator may ask the patient if he or any of his relatives have had chronic bronchitis. Unfortunately, since this seems to be a genetic problem, there seems little chance of a treatment or cure. Also, if a child were to be conceived by a male with this defect, the child might also suffer from it.

ABSENCE OF SPERM IN THE EJACULATE

Around 5 to 10 percent of men have to be told the tragic news that there are no sperm in their ejaculates. In earlier chapters we discussed two causes of azoospermia (literally, the absence of sperm): obstruction after infection in the tubes carrying the sperm out of the testicles; and a condition called Sertoli cell only syndrome, in which the germ cells have failed to migrate into the testicles before birth. Another cause is that for some inexplicable reason, the sperm production lines have suddenly stopped. At what stage they have stopped varies from one group of patients to another. The cause could be a virus, a faulty chromosome, a missing and as yet unidentified hormone or a sperm chemical. The testicular biopsy reveals everything but the original cause. One of the most frequent sex chromosome faults in men is Klinefelter's syndrome, in which each cell has an extra X chromosome. Although many of these men can look quite normal, their testicles and especially the sperm factories in their testicles self-destruct around puberty. The result is that the tubes become filled with a tangled network of fibers that cause the testicles to shrink. For these and other azoospermic men, the only possible choice is donor insemination or adoption.

UNDESCENDED TESTICLES

Failure of the testicles to descend into the scrotum after birth is not a rare occurrence. The problem is that even when corrected before the age of five it is often associated with infertility. In fact, even in men where only one testicle has failed to descend, 35 percent will suffer infertility despite correction of the problem at an early age. It seems that other faults in the reproductive apparatus are associated with these problems of testicle descent. One such fault is the obstruction of the various tubes, which explains why the later semen samples are so poor.

The causes of male infertility are many and often complex. The major problem for the fertility specialist is that there are only three conditions that can be treated with any reasonable chance of success: hormone disturbances, infection, and varicocele. Men whose infertility is caused by other factors may go desperate rounds with acupuncturists, faith healers, and homeopaths before the tragic truth can be swallowed. The most frustrating group of men for the specialist are those who appear to be completely normal—both they and their wives have high fertility scores—but for some inexplicable reason fertilization does not occur. It's clear that there is still a long way to go before scientists can fully understand the conditions that must be fulfilled to accomplish a pregnancy. The new techniques of in vitro fertilization are helping us understand which properties of the sperm are necessary for it to penetrate the egg. The new generation of sperm machines is increasing our awareness of the impact of the environment, of drugs, and of life-style on sperm quality. We are also entering a new era in our understanding of the plight of the barren couple, the contribution that the man makes to the dilemma, the psychology of being infertile, and the recognition of this condition as a bona fide sickness entitled to the full attention of the research community and the sympathy of the general population.

18 STRESS: NATURE'S CONTRACEPTIVE

Stress is a term that is almost impossible to define—at least to the satisfaction of those whose lives it touches. Maybe this is because it embraces so many of life's different situations and because our response to it appears to be so interwoven into the fabric of our personalities. But for our earliest ancestors, the definition was clear: stress was staring into the jaws of a hungry lion, or surviving periods of drought and famine when the climate changed for the worst. Stress was being socially isolated from the rest of the group, or having to fight for space when the population became too large. Such periods of adversity were hardly suitable times for bringing offspring into the world. Nature had foreseen this problem by programing those primitive brains to release chemical signals that could switch off the reproductive process just long enough until the threat to the animal's survival had passed. Millions of years later, the specter of the hungry lion still haunts our daily lives—an imaginary finger poised over the same chemical switch ready to slow down or turn off our testicles—a primitive response to events that our bodies misinterpret as being life threatening. We may be grinding our teeth in a traffic jam or running a marathon. We could be grieving over the loss of a loved one or worrying about how we are going to pay all the bills. Each of these situations can provoke in us, to different degrees, the same type of reaction our ancestors experienced when life was relatively less complicated but at times infinitely more dangerous.

Let us consider an activity that for some is stress in its most extreme form: exercise. Mere mention of the word can strike fear into the hearts of many, and the threat of having to do it is sufficient to induce remarkable changes in the body's chemistry. Researchers have known for some time that women athletes often suffer from irregular or abnormal menstrual cycles. The harder the woman trains, the greater the disturbance and in some cases it can lead to a full cessation of menstruation. This can mean only one thing—that the delicate balance of the sex chemicals responsible for the monthly changes in their inner sex organs is being disturbed.

After reading about these findings, it is not surprising to hear that young, talented girls who begin with intense physical exercise or training before the onset of menstruation often show a delay in puberty. The most extreme cases have been seen in Olympic gymnasts and ballet dancers who, in addition, also have the tough pressure of competition on their young shoulders, with all the mental frustration that involves.

Men, of course, do not menstruate but they do show disturbances in the masculine equivalents of the female sex hormones and organs. The stress of long-distance running has been shown to send testosterone levels spiraling downward. The same thing happens when healthy young men get their first experience of heavy combat training after enlistment. This is a poor testament to the typical propaganda used for attracting professional soldiers: "Be a man and join the army!" Many other forms of physical stress, such as undergoing major surgery, suffering serious burns, or surviving a major heart attack, can also temporarily shut down the functioning of our sex glands. Of course, as we will see, many of these situations also involve extreme mental anguish, which also takes its toll.

How does our body reduce the activity of our sex organs when we are threatened in this way? It appears to do so by pressing one or all of several hormonal switches, all of which serve to dampen or turn off our fertility, but in different ways. About ten years ago, scientists discovered that our body produces its own pain-killers—biological sedatives very much like morphine. They showed that these natural drugs increase in our brains when we are threatened by pain or injury. In pregnant women they increased, as one might expect, around the time of labor. Acupuncture was shown to stimulate their release, thus explaining at least one of its anesthetic effects. The study of these natural pain-killers also helped scientists understand more about one of nature's puzzles: how some people could survive terrifying injuries like amputation of arms and legs without apparently suffering agony, and how some animals could be literally eaten alive without showing great suffering.

Recently, these pain-killers were shown to increase in marathon runners not only during but before the race, and in untrained volunteers during intense exercise. Maybe this explains the euphoria that can be experienced by athletes after particularly grueling races, as well as the fact that some joggers become "addicted" to regular activity just as others can be dependent on shots of morphine. What makes these pain-killers so interesting is that they also have other dramatic effects on our body chemistry—reducing the amounts of the hormones controlling the activity of the testicles and ovaries. The result is that this natural "morphine" not only buffers our bodies from eventual pain caused by the stress, but also reduces the chance that our offspring will experience the same pain by denying their chance for existence.

Other channels through which stress can exert such a contraceptive effect have been known for many years, the most obvious involving the adrenal gland, a powerhouse of a gland that spews out a chemical dynamite when we experience stress. These stress chemicals have also been shown to inhibit our fertility, an extra piece of security if our pain-killers fail to play their contraceptive role. Recently, scientists have discovered that stress nerves also have direct connections with the Leydig cells, which explains why acute stress can so quickly send our testosterone levels plummeting.

But stress need not be experienced only as physical. Psychological stress can be just as real and in some cases even more ominous. The evidence that psychological stress stamps its mark on the male sexual organs is impressive. The first documented work on its effects on the number of sperm we produce was a study of prisoners sentenced to death and kept waiting a long time before execution. Small pieces of their testicles were removed by enthusiastic research workers at regular intervals before the big day arrived. They saw that the sperm factories in the testicles gradually began to slow their production and in some cases came to an absolute stop. A valid question is whether it was the threat of execution or the visits from these eager scientists that made them perspire and gave them palpitations. Although there are stressful situations that could, by some, be considered equivalent to waiting on death row—waiting for letters from the tax collector or a visit from the in-laws—few men will ever experience such a degree of psychological stress. On the other hand, milder forms of psychological stress are widespread in today's society and these too have effects on fertility. In 1806, an English doctor suggested that stress caused by a change in social status could influence a person's sex glands and lower his fertility. He argued that a fall in social status or even the fear of falling in social status was enough to make a man impotent. In his own time he was laughed at for these ideas; today he would be written up in medical journals.

Studies of apes have shown that those unfortunates at the bottom of the social hierarchy have lower levels of the male hormone, testosterone, than those higher up. They also get a lousy deal when it comes to the mating game. In contrast, the high-ranking male, who is literally overflowing with male hormone, has the choice of the females and rarely suffers the shame of a weak erection. The same has been observed in female hierarchies in which the lower the animal's status the more irregular their sexual cycle and the greater the fertility problem.

Similar studies have never been carried out in our fellow human beings partly because there are few situations in which such a stable male hierarchy exists. One interesting possibility is the hierarchy seen in large corporate industries, where the ranking order on the way up to the chairman of the board is often clearcut, and where the constant fear of losing one's job in the lower ranks must be a normal feature of everyday life. It has been written that in a stable family situation, one of the first symptoms of a problem at work is when a man or a woman loses interest in sex—is this the first sign that our primitive reflex is being awakened?

Interestingly, depending where on the social scale monkeys sit, the reactions to stress may be quite different. Whereas those at the bottom of the scale react by switching off their sex organs, those at the top of the scale actually appear to thrive on stress and react by actually increasing their male hormone levels. An analogy has been made for Type A and Type B individuals in human societies. The aggressive competitive Type A man reacts to psychological stress in a positive way, whereas stress for the more neutral and emotionally stable Type B person sends his male sex hormone level falling in the opposite direction. Such analogies are interesting but as yet have a weak foundation in fact.

What about other forms of psychological stress? Everybody has heard about sperm banks, but what most people do not know is that most of the *deposits* are made by students who differ from their fellow human beings in having to endure at regular intervals throughout the year stress in its most modern form: examinations. Sperm banks in England claim that they can tell when this dreaded time is approaching by a marked decline in sperm counts.

When intellectual stress can worm its way into our reproductive processes it is easy to understand why some gynecologists feel that emotional stress may explain why some couples have problems conceiving. As recently as fifteen years ago some doctors believed that emotional factors caused 40 percent of all cases of infertility. Today the figure is believed closer to 5 percent. On the other hand, it is generally agreed that if a man or woman has reduced fertility, the emotional conflicts and feelings of desperation associated with this condition can make matters even worse—reducing the chances of conceiving even further. Several studies have shown that in some cases when a couple have finally come to terms with their infertile state and adopted a child, it's not long before the stress-free couple is expecting its own child.

Finally, let us consider an even more ominous aspect of this relationship between stress and our sexuality. It has been known for some time that at very precise periods in pregnancy the baby's body is molded into a male or female direction—such changes are necessary for us to show normal male or female sexual behavior as adults. In the baby boy's case, at these precise times there is a sudden surge of testosterone. In animal studies it has been shown that stressing the mother at these precise times can turn off this surge in male hormone, and the consequences of this are dramatic. The resulting offspring show abnormal sexual behavior, some cannot or will not perform the sexual act, and many lead disorganized sexual lives. No equivalent study has been carried out in humans, but the implications raised by these animal studies, especially when we consider the levels of stress that a pregnant woman can be subjected to in modern society, are apparent.

Stress is an integral part of our lives but the next time you are cursing at your fellow human beings in a traffic jam or at work, pause for a while and look over your shoulder. The hungry lion is poised to sink its teeth and claws into an area of your body you least expected!

19 VASECTOMY: THE SHORTCUT TO CONTRACEPTION

Most men are endowed with two factories between their legs that spew out millions of little blueprints of themselves day and night, all eager to go to work on an egg. The only road out from these pulsating production lines to the outside world are two muscular tubes called the vas deferens. About 14 inches long with a hole about 0.2 inches wide, these tubes chart a tortuous course from their source up and around, under the bladder where they plug into the prostate gland. Even with their nerves cut, these tubes are in constant movement; in fact, up to twenty-four hours after death the vas deferens may still be wiggling about—a sobering thought! During an ejaculation, nerves fire off tidal waves of contractions sending little packets of sperm to far off destinations. If anything squeezes or clogs up these little motorways the result is sterility. Some men are born without them or with bits missing from them. Other men suffer blockages of the vas deferens due to infections. And each year, thousands of men in countries throughout the world have these tubes cut and separated by the surgeon's knife.

Before vasectomies became fashionable, the only way a man could do his bit for population control was to wear a condom or practice abstinence. The condom became a symbol that the man was in control. Those little oval packets, carried discreetly by gentlemen in made-to-measure compartments in their wallets, were membership cards to an exclusive male club. As long as they didn't look too worn at the edges it was clear evidence to his comrades-in-arms that he was a male always on the hunt. Not only that, they were a guarantee of success once the prey had been cornered. But then came the pill, and for the first time in the history of sex, women became in charge. In the early stages, men fought hard not to lose the advantage—spreading rumors that the pill was poison, that it led to mental instability, or gave women hairy chests—but to no avail. The only way to be master of the bedroom once again was to succumb to the scalpel and get sterilized or, more correctly, get vasectomized. Now it was suddenly, "You trust me and I'll trust you." The problem for the hunting male was to convince his potential conquests that he really was "safe." He could, of course, lower his trousers and show her his two tiny white battle scars, but this is hardly acceptable behavior in a restaurant or discotheque. No, he had to have a strategically placed neon flashing light. In England, the "vasectomy tie" was the answer. Worn only by sterilized males who could document the operation, the special symbols on this tie were a seal of guarantee: here was a man to be trusted. Everything went well until black-market copies began appearing by the thousands on every street corner, forcing women to play a dangerous form of Russian roulette with only a minority of men firing blanks.

For the married couple the situation was different. A woman could now boast proudly that her man took his contraceptive responsibility seriously—sacrificing a few centimeters of his anatomy just for her. The problem is that today, with safer contraceptive pills and simpler ways of sterilizing women, this chivalrous behavior is once again going the way of the dinosaurs, at least in certain lands.

THE HISTORY OF THE VASECTOMY

When did vasectomy first begin? Obviously, not before somebody invented an anesthetic; a man may have noble ideas but he's not stupid. He had to wait until the early 1900s. Actually the first vasectomies were not done to limit the spread of the human race but to limit the spread of infection. Surgeons operating on men's sex glands often saw infection spreading from their not-so-sterile scalpels down the vas deferens to the testicles, rather like igniting a thin line of gunpowder and watching the barrel hit the roof. With a stroke of brilliance, they cut the tubes to stop the infection in its tracks.

In the 1920s and 1930s, still no one had really seen or promoted the vasectomy's potential as a form of contraception. Instead, the operation was recommended by a number of eccentric scientists as a way of recapturing lost youth, of curing impotence, and of reversing senility. The idea was that by shutting off this constant leakage of testicular juices, they could preserve and increase sexual strength. One scientist traveled around proudly showing before and after photographs of old dogs becoming rampant puppies again. Certainly, the operation suddenly became attractive to great numbers of elderly men. A little later, as antibiotics and local pain-killers gradually came into the picture, men began knocking on the surgeon's door to use the operation to make them sterile. Any positive side effects on potency were presumably accepted with a smile.

In the 1930s, the specter of involuntary sterilization raised its ugly head. Suddenly men had no choice—you either lose your testicles or get your cords cut! In Germany, in 1933 alone, 28,000 civilian Jews were subjected to such surgery in the name of "race improvement." Thankfully today, the majority of European countries have made laws forbidding this type of forced sterilization. In the postwar years, the operation spread first to Japan and Korea, and then eastward to California and westward to India. In those years, a heated topic of discussion was the population explosion, and there were gloomy forebodings about the future.

India was one third-world country that overreacted. First they used bribery—a free transistor radio was given to each man voluntarily getting his cords cut. Later, as it became more impatient, the Indian government decided to skip the radios and use other less subtle forms of persuasion. In Maharashtra in 1976, it was proposed that men with more than two children who refused the operation be jailed for two years. In 1976, the Indian government proudly reported seven million vasectomies had been carried out, earning them great international acclaim. But the people in the street began to get tired of running from the sterilization squads, and in the next general election, Mrs. Gandhi's Congress Party suffered a crushing defeat at the polls, presumably brought to their knees by the few remaining men with their tubes still intact. Elsewhere in the 1950s and 1960s, men brushed aside the primitive associations and taboos associated with operations on their precious sexual equipment and gradually embraced vasectomy as an attractive method of permanent birth control.

Jones told the doctor he wanted a vasectomy. "All right," said the medic, "but have you discussed the operation and its implications with your wife and family?" "Yes," said the man. "I'm not really thrilled about it, but my wife asked the children to vote on it." "What was the outcome?" asked the doctor. "The kids favored it, eleven to three."

CLIPPED, CLOGGED, OR TIED?

The actual operation is very easily completed. You can feel the vas deferens as they leave the scrotum as two thickened cords. A local anesthesia, a snip here and a couple of knots there, and—bingo—you are a 100 percent sterile male. In China, the procedure has been even more simplified—the so-called bloodless vasectomy—in which everything is done through a single hole less than half an inch long.

To be on the safe side, the surgeon performing a vasectomy removes about a quarter of an inch of both tubes and squeezes them out onto a microscope slide. The surgeon wants to see sperm under the microscope (as opposed to blood, which means he's clipped a blood vessel) to ensure that he has indeed cut the vas deferens. This precaution will help prevent lawyers whose clients (the surgeon's patients) have conceived a child. However, if the subject does become a father in spite of the operation, it may not necessarily be because the doctor has unknowingly removed bits of a blood vessel. A major problem is that these tubes sometimes have an uncanny ability to reconnect even when a large chunk is removed! In fact, the open ends are often folded back on themselves to reduce that possibility. Plugging them, tying them with string, crushing them, pinching them closed with metal clips, or even cutting and burning the open ends are no guarantee that the supply lines will not be reopened in a few months. The greatest concern is that the doctor always has to have in the back of his mind the possibility that the patient may change his mind in a couple of years and want to reverse the procedure. If the tubes are cut too short during the vasectomy, and the patient wants the operation reversed, he may have to go through life with a slight forward tilt.

SIDE EFFECTS OF VASECTOMY

For most men, the big questions about vasectomy concern the side effects: Will I become impotent and will it make my penis or testicles shrink? The good news is that potency is not affected—if the man was motivated from the start and didn't have nervous problems or doubts about his masculinity before the operation. And, no, the testicles will not shrink or fall off. In fact they appear to be in full production, just as if nothing had happened. Sure, the reservoirs of sperm in the epididymis become swollen almost to bursting, but it appears that little armies of scavenger cells are mobilized to mop up all of the sperm cells that died waiting for a journey that would never happen. The semen volume doesn't change because so little of the ejaculate comes from the testicles under normal conditions. And finally, the news everybody is waiting for: No, the male organ does not shrink after vasectomy.

One possible side effect that should be considered and discussed with your physician before undergoing a vasectomy involves antibodies and the immune system. It has been known for some time that seven to ten days after a vasectomy, and in approximately half of the men operated on, antibodies directed against their own sperm cells begin to appear in the blood. As previously discussed (see page 184), sperm cells are so unlike normal body cells that the immune system will attack them if given the chance and create antibodies. Normally this does not happen because the sperm cells and these attack units are separated by a barrier. After vasectomy, this barrier apparently breaks down. Since the antibodies, which can cause the sperm to clump together, can circulate in the body for many years, a problem can arise if a sterile man decides he wants to make babies again. Even if he can be reconnected, the sperm that do find their way out may be covered with a sticky mass of antibodies that can prevent them from reaching the egg, thus causing infertility.

GETTING UNTIED

Divorce was not talked about much in the 1950s. Once a man had his tubes knotted it was usually for life. But just as the surgeons finally got the hang of keeping the ends of the vas deferens apart, men began to change their minds and wanted them to join the ends together again. And as the divorce rate increased and men found new partners, the demands for reversing the operation also increased. This created a dilemma for the physician. It was a lot easier cutting the tubes than connecting them. Researchers began to talk of implanting little on-off valves in the tubes that could be changed by a simple surgical procedure. It looked good on paper. Today, having a successful reversal depends on whether the surgeon uses a knife and fork or a microscope. With the proper technique involving microsurgery, some surgeons can boast up to 60 to 80 percent pregnancies after the operation.

Vasectomy remains today the simplest, most effective, least harmful way of making a man sterile with a reasonable chance of reversal. Maybe it's time for modern man to grit his teeth and at least share the burden of contraception, which for so long has been placed on the shoulders of his partner.

WHAT ABOUT THE MALE PILL?

Since the 1960s the pressure on scientists to create an efficient form of male contraception has been extremely intense. The recent rise in feminism certainly helped to increase the pressure, but the results have been disappointing and have done little to relieve it. Unfortunately, it is a fact of life that the reproductive processes in the male are more complicated than those in the female. It's not that we have to prevent the release of one egg but that we have to stop the release of 200 million sperm, and you need only one to cause a pregnancy. Also, the hormone responsible for giving a man his sex drive and erection is the same one necessary for making the sperm. If this hormone is disturbed, then so is a man's sex desire and sex life.

How has man's ingenuity tackled the problem? Many hormonal contraceptives have been tried over the last twenty years but none has led to a breakthrough. The finding that the male sex hormone testosterone could inhibit sperm production just as the female sex hormones, progesterone and estrogen, could inhibit ovulation, prompted some to advocate a testosterone pill. Large amounts of testosterone in the blood inhibit the release of the luteinizing hormone (LH), which shuts down the Leydig cells in the testicles. It is this locally produced testosterone in the testicle that is responsible for stimulating sperm production. In the early stages it had to be injected, something the bravest man would think twice about. Today, there are testosterone pills, which work fine if the man can remember to take them regularly. Athletes taking the synthetic forms of testosterone, anabolic steroids, are in the majority of cases sterile because of their effects on LH. But there was also talk about possible links with arteriosclerosis. The encouraging news is that new and better testosterone pills are on the horizon with doses that do not seem to interfere with blood cholesterol levels or clotting factors.

Other hormones were tried, including female hormones, but the hardy volunteers complained of night sweating, the development of breasts, and impotence. Maybe it is with understandable cynicism that men read in the popular press about research on yet another revolutionary male pill. An interesting possibility that appeared roughly ten years ago involved the use of a naturally occurring brain hormone. This small molecule was found to switch off testicular function and could be administered in the form of a nasal spray. Presumably this restricted its use to men without colds and hayfever. The fact that testosterone production was also switched off meant that men would rapidly become impotent and therefore the spray had to be used in conjunction with the testosterone pill with all the problems that involved.

One form of oral contraception that attracted the attention of both scientists and the popular press in the late 1980s is a compound isolated from cotton seed oil. It has been described as having almost no side effects, complete reversibility, and extremely high efficiency without affecting sexual desire or the ability to have an erection. It was first discovered after men in a certain area of China complained of sterility after having their food fried in the oil. Scientists soon isolated the active ingredient and trials on thousands of Chinese men at that time were extremely encouraging. Today, information from Western scientists indicates an unacceptable level of toxicity to normal cells in the body, so that an alteration in the structure of the molecule appears to be needed. Whether this will be the male pill men have been waiting for, only time will tell. At least women may hopefully gain some satisfaction that something is being done to encourage men to share the burden of contraception.

INDEX